Praise for *My Battlefield, Your Office*

Justin spoke at our annual leadership conference to approximately 2,000 of our managers and supervisors. Had this book been published then, we would have bought one for everyone there. *My Battlefield, Your Office* captures Justin's real world experience in a way that is educational and a pleasure to read.

— Chuck Rubin, CEO, Michaels

Justin deserves our thanks for his service to our country and for providing his leadership lessons from the front lines. *My Battlefield, Your Office* is a great resource to help managers become leaders. Justin's personal account of his own triumph over tragedy is an absorbing and inspiring story that enhances his key leadership takeaways, making this a "must read" book.

— William M. Klepper, PhD, Management Professor and Academic Director, Executive Education, Columbia Business School

We all benefit when great ideas are shared. Each chapter of *My Battlefield, Your Office* is powerful in its own way, and Justin provides us with insightful, thoughtful and useful lessons to make us better. Any management team will certainly benefit from reading this book and implementing its lessons and guidance.

— Bethany Coates, Assistant Dean, Global Innovation Programs, Stanford Graduate School of Business

Justin spoke at our 2014 National Conference in front of over 1,200 managers, corporate partners and senior leaders. His theme of "Officers Eat Last" aligned perfectly with our conference theme while delivering valuable insight to our leadership team. *My Battlefield, Your Office* really takes his work to the next level in a way that will resonate with all levels of leaders.

— Wayne Goldberg, President  *tes*

Justin's heroic personal story is incre lps
us understand what it takes to motiv
Leading people is always going to be challenging, but Justin just made it a whole lot easier. With real life experiences, powerful quotes and stories, Justin masterfully describes what it takes to be a leader anyone

would want to follow. As a general officer in the U.S. Army, I have certainly read many books about leadership and this is one I am proud to wholeheartedly endorse.

— Mark A. Graham, Major General, U.S. Army (Retired)

Justin's personal story is a testament to the power of the human spirit. He gave an unforgettable address at our December 2012 commencement that deeply moved all in attendance and earned a spontaneous standing ovation. Justin's life, and this book, provide powerful lessons about teamwork, resilience, and our human capacity to overcome obstacles of all kinds. *My Battlefield, Your Office* provides important perspectives on the challenges we confront in organizations of all types, and most of all on how to work with and motivate people.

— Jonathan R. Alger, President, James Madison University

My Battlefield, Your Office is an inspiring true story full of courage, commitment, and motivation to achieve your best even under the most difficult circumstances. Justin's advice from real life experiences is invaluable to anyone in a leadership position or aspiring to be a leader. If you are looking for inspiration and motivation with down-to-earth lessons on leadership, then this is the book for you!

— Bob Nardelli, Founder and CEO of XLR-8 and former Chairman and CEO of Chrysler and Home Depot

Through the story of his military journey, Justin represents the voices of the very best that America has to offer and he does a fantastic job. A powerful and inspirational speaker, I am thrilled that Justin has now written *My Battlefield, Your Office*. His personal message of dedication, perseverance, and triumph against nearly impossible odds will resonate with every reader, just as his leadership lessons will too.

— James Barclay, Lieutenant General, U.S. Army (Retired)

Justin demonstrates that succeeding in business and in life requires character, determination, vision, and compassion. I particularly enjoyed the personal stories that Justin shared with us in *My Battlefield, Your Office*, and it is obvious to me how this book will help so many managers and supervisors who did not have the benefit of Justin's experience during their own training.

— Miguel Howe, Colonel, U.S. Army (Retired), Director, Military Service Institute, George W. Bush Presidential Center

If you are serious about being a truly impactful leader, *My Battlefield, Your Office* is a must. It will demonstrate to you how to get the most out of your people, and to be a valuable resource to everyone around. On top of that, it encourages us to embrace a healthy work-life balance and to be great citizens! Justin has so much to offer, and I am confident this book is the springboard for exciting things to follow.

— Eric Eversole, Vice President, US Chamber of Commerce;
President, Hiring Our Heroes

I have known Justin for a number of years now and fully understand why he is a leader in the veteran community. No organization teaches leadership like the Marine Corps, and Justin has translated those valuable lessons into a must-read book for any manager or supervisor. For the millions of managers across our country who worked hard and were promoted without ever learning the right way to lead people, they now have a great resource to help them do just that. Through the story of his military journey, Justin represents the voices of the very best that America has to offer. A powerful and inspirational speaker, Justin's personal message of dedication, perseverance, and triumph against nearly impossible odds will resonate with every reader, as will his leadership lessons.

— Richard Jones, Executive Vice President and General Tax Counsel,
CBS Corporation

My Battlefield, Your Office vividly captures Justin's personal challenges and his will to both survive and thrive as a leader and as a living example of resilience. It's inspirational."

— Gerry Byrne, Vice Chairman, Penske Media Corporation
(USMC Captain 1966-1969)

As a father, the highest compliment I can pay someone is to let them know if I found something extremely valuable, I would share it with my son. Justin's story, mental and physical toughness, and lessons learned is one of my top recommendations for my son's reading list. A must read for all Americans.

— James Schenck, President and CEO, Pentagon Federal Credit Union

My Battlefield, Your Office

Leadership Lessons from the Front Lines

Justin Constantine

Lieutenant Colonel (ret), U.S. Marine Corps

Nobody teaches leadership better than the Marine Corps, and I had the benefit of living and breathing their basic leadership principles over a significant portion of my life. This book is dedicated to the millions of other managers and supervisors who are hardworking employees, but never learned how to productively lead people along the way.

ACKNOWLEDGMENTS

I specifically want to thank my wife, Dahlia Constantine, for helping me in every aspect of this book. Dahlia was the cornerstone of my successful recovery after a tough day in Iraq, and through her selfless support I am now in a position to help others with life's challenges. Further, I also want to thank both of my parents. My mother taught me so much about customer service and good business practices while helping me with my landscaping company and paper route as a young boy. And my father never tired of running through ideas with me across the kitchen table. Finally, I want to thank JJ McKeever, who spent many hours with me making this book a reality – he helped me gather my ideas together in a cohesive manner and rounded out the concepts with great examples from his life experiences.

Contents

Captain Constantine crossing a channel in Iraq. This was our typical uniform along with 65 pounds of protective armor.

CHAPTER 1

WHO I AM AND WHY THAT MATTERS

I CANNOT SEE OUT of my left eye. I am missing most of my teeth and the end of my tongue. I cannot run—the doctors removed several of the bones in my legs to use in reconstructing my upper and lower jaws. When I speak in front of an audience, I do not speak "normally." I also suffer from post-traumatic stress (PTS) and a traumatic brain injury.

So, why am I writing a book?

To turn around one of F. Scott Fitzgerald's more infamous lines, I can tell you that there are indeed many "second acts in American life." I am living proof of that.

And I am incredibly humbled by all that I went through. You see, the injury that resulted in all of the maladies I stated above happened when I was a major in the United States Marine Corps. During a combat mission in Iraq, a sniper's bullet entered my skull just behind my left ear and exited out of my mouth, missing my spinal cord but still causing catastrophic damage. I retired as a lieutenant colonel.

After a continuous campaign of operations and rehab, I have taken the lessons I learned in the Marines, and the lessons I have learned from my recovery, and applied them to the corporate business world. Leading a team in the military and leading a team in the private or public sector have definite parallels. I often speak on management and leadership and, from those speaking engagements, all levels of management have asked me to bring out a book to complement and reinforce the principles I talk about. This book is my response to those requests, and I hope you enjoy the result. Believe me, writing this book is another milestone that I am thankful to have had the opportunity to even attempt, let alone accomplish, since my injury.

To give you a little background on how I got to this point, I joined the Marine Corps after my second year of law school. However, when I deployed to Iraq in 2006, it was not in the role of a JAG officer. In the Marine Corps, all the officers learn the basics of many different jobs, so I volunteered for deployment as a civil affairs team leader. In that role, I had the honor of leading a team of eight Marines and a Navy corpsman as part of a Marine infantry battalion located halfway between Fallujah and Ramadi in Al Anbar Province. As a civil affairs officer, I was to develop contacts and contracts with the local population to help rebuild the basic infrastructure needed for any city: clean running water, functioning electricity, drivable roads, and much-needed schools.

Unfortunately for so many warriors serving at that time, the fall of 2006 was an extremely volatile time in Iraq, and the insurgency there was at the height of its power. Convincing the local Iraqis to work with us to rebuild their cities was virtually impossible. By day, we would be advocating for what they needed and how we wanted to help. By night, members of the insurgency would visit them with death threats if they cooperated with us. In short, I guess you could say that the enemy's negative P.R. campaign had more of an impact than our positive strategy to help rebuild.

Despite the difficulties, that experience certainly gave me a unique understanding as to how to build consensus among people with competing, to say the least, objectives, and how to utilize my staff to the best of their abilities in such an environment. There were definitely obstacles, but I will always look back on the time I spent in Iraq as the highlight of my career. Not too many other lawyers get to lead Marines in a combat environment, and I learned a lot about effective leadership, and about myself, while I was there.

Because I worked closely with the battalion commander, he put me on his "jump team." This was comprised of about a dozen Marines. That team went out "across the wire" together about four or five times per week. This meant that we left the base and ventured into places where the opposition might be established or entrenched. We were on a regular combat patrol on October 18, 2006, and we had just gotten to an area where we knew an enemy sniper was active: He had already killed a few Marines.

We actually had a reporter with us that day. Through later conversations with that reporter, my brothers-in-arms, and some of the doctors that treated and saved me, I learned what happened that day—I do not remember most of it, only snapshots here and there for the next few weeks. I remember our patrol brief that morning, and then waking up almost a week later on an airplane. From their stories, I know that earlier that day, we stopped at an Iraqi police station that had been shot up by insurgents the night before. We wanted to show the Iraqi police how to defend their position better. We also had stopped at one of our forward operating bases to check on our Marines, and I remember noticing, then, that the reporter was kind of just standing around—an easy target for a sniper. When we got out of the vehicle at our next stop and started walking away from the Humvee, I told him that he needed to move faster or that he might get shot. Based on that, he took a big step forward, just before a round came in right where his head had been and hit the wall next to us. Before I could react, the next shot hit me behind my left ear and exited out my mouth, destroying the bone and soft tissue on the left side of my face, though missing my spinal cord and brain.

Fortunately for me, Corpsman George Grant is an amazing young man. As blood was pouring out of my head and what remained of my face, he performed rescue breathing and an emergency tracheotomy on me. While the sniper was still shooting at us, in fact also shooting the Marine behind me, Corpsman Grant saved my life. He was also wearing 65 pounds of protective armor, like we all were that summer, so it was difficult for him to move around in small spaces. And like all of us, George was sweating like crazy because it was over 100 degrees in the desert that day. As torn up as my face was, George breathed for me, performing a battlefield tracheotomy so that I would not drown in my own blood. In the face of overwhelming adversity, and with complete disregard for his own life, George was able to focus entirely on me and keep me alive. In the face of the absolute chaos going on around us, he conducted such a perfect tracheotomy that my plastic surgeon at the military hospital thought another surgeon had performed it.

In fact, George had never performed a surgery like that on a human before. He had only performed it once in a training environment for Navy corpsmen at Camp Pendleton, California. He actually performed that same operation on a pig—I do not know what this says about me, but the pig survived and so did I!

When I was shot, the commanding officer of the infantry battalion, a lieutenant colonel named Todd Desgrosseilliers from Newport, Rhode Island, was faced with a tough choice. He could either call in an emergency airlift and wait for the helicopter or have me driven to the nearest aid station in an effort to stabilize me. The problem with the helicopter option was that Lieutenant Colonel Desgrosseilliers had no idea how long it would take due to the competing priorities for choppers on the battlefield. The danger with driving was the ever-present risk of roadside bombs.

Improvised explosive devices (IEDs) are incredibly powerful weapons, and we dealt with them every single day, as anyone who watched the national news at the time knows. In fact, when I checked in with Lieutenant Colonel Desgrosseilliers when I first got to Iraq, I saw the pictures of all the young Marines from the battalion who had already been killed. They were so young it looked like a page from a high school yearbook, and most of their untimely deaths were from those IEDs.

Lieutenant Colonel Desgrosseilliers quickly made the command decision. He opted to have Corporal Jordan Buhler, a young Marine from a rural town outside New Orleans, drive me to the Shock Trauma Platoon at Al-Taqaddum Air Base (commonly referred to as "TQ") forward aid station and he told him to drive as fast as possible.

Driving 70 miles an hour is no big deal in the states on a highway. But in Iraq, we drove much slower wherever we went, scanning for roadside bombs the entire time. In fact, we had a standing order to never drive faster than 15 miles per hour. We had learned the hard way that hitting one of those IEDs while going faster than that drastically increased the chances of the vehicle flipping end-over-end upon impact, which would probably kill everyone inside. However, just as Corpsman Grant had done minutes earlier, Corporal Buhler put his life on the line for me without a second thought. He drove 70 miles per hour to the aid station to ensure I got there within "the golden hour," the time period that is so critical after such a traumatic injury.

I am sure that George Grant and Jordon Buhler did not wake up on October 18, 2006, planning to save my life. They simply reacted to the situation around them. They fell back on who they were at their cores—compassionate, selfless, faithful, and committed to the greater good. And they fell back on their training, the training that reinforced and enhanced those core values.

I know that I will never be the Marine I once was. My career as a trial lawyer is over. I know that I will now, and for the rest of my life, have problems eating, drinking, speaking, and just remembering things. Those obstacles are something I deal with every day, but I still consider myself one of the luckiest people alive. In fact, I think it is because of the injury that caused those problems that I am far closer with my wife, Dahlia, than I would have thought possible. I now know that I am far stronger than I ever could have imagined, and I can put everyday obstacles into their proper perspective, focusing instead on what is truly important to Dahlia and me. Winston Churchill said, "Never give in. Never give in. Never. Never. Never." I fully embraced that philosophy during my recovery, and I apply that mantra to all I do now.

The original reason for this book is that I now have a career as an inspirational speaker and leadership advisor. From the feedback I've gotten from my speaking engagements, at which my primary audience has been the business community of America, I have found that many of the practices I preach to mid-level managers and CEOs alike are practices ingrained in me during my military training and experiences leading others in relative peace and in combat. I will be discussing in detail in this book how these lessons from the military are very important for and easily applicable to running a team, a division, or an entire company.

While any instruction I give pertains to all levels of an organization, I believe I mainly speak to those in middle management, particularly those who were promoted into their current leadership positions without the benefit of formal leadership training. My career as an officer in the Marine Corps ran along the lines of middle management: I needed to get the most out of the limited personnel around me and I needed my subordinates to know that, in me, they had a leader they could trust and depend upon.

In my experiences in leadership and in speaking to and with those in leadership, it seems that one of the problems within most hierarchical structures in corporate America is that a leader is usually perceived as a person who would say to those under him, "What have you done for me lately?" This may be the impression people have of our various armed services, especially if they never had personal contact with the military. That is not even close to the truth. Anyone who goes through any type of leadership training in the military learns that, while meeting an objective is important, it is just as important to care for the personnel under you.

In the speeches I have given to date, audiences have been very receptive to this notion. The United States of America still has the most powerful economy in the world. Our standard of living is high and I like to think that the country still offers boundless opportunities for anyone willing to work hard. True, there have been some rips in the fabric of corporate America in recent years. But we do have companies whose overriding concern for the bottom line has had an impact on personnel decisions. Loyalty to "your" company, and vice-versa, is becoming a thing of the past, a lost quality, in many cases. But it does not have to be this way.

What I want the reader to glean from this book is that the way that management goes about managing can foster success for the company and for everyone who works for it. These are lessons I learned through my training and through practical application in the Marines. And these are lessons I saw in the practice of others and that I saw in my own actions during my extensive recovery.

I believe that a company manager who truly wants to be successful will not go wrong by applying these lessons of leadership. The military has proven to be a consistently effective organization over the course of the history of the United States. If you look at the leadership lessons that an examination of the military provides on a scientific level, there is a wealth of facts and case studies that explain and support that success. Plus, military leadership has also been tested in the greatest of all laboratories: the battlefield. Corporate management uses military terminology a great deal in the boardroom and even more on the production floor. So I think it is only fitting that corporate leadership should apply the military's hard-won lessons to their own efforts to achieve lasting success.

I really enjoy what I do for a living. I know that my mentors will always have my back, and that both encourages and inspires me to keep working. I get excited when I get to work on my speeches and I got excited when I decided to tackle this book project. I believe that what I have learned by my experience overcoming adversity can positively influence others around me. Nothing would make me happier than knowing that I helped someone overcome some challenge in their management position. In the military, we are constantly taught to do our job, to do it well, and to determine how the simple act of doing our own job helps or could help those working next to us. Can you imagine how vibrant all of our companies would be if people took it upon themselves to adhere to that simple philosophy? Everyone in a leadership position can make that happen!

In some of my speeches, I refer to Major Douglas Alexander Zembiec and something he said. Major Zembiec was an officer in the United States Marine Corps and is often referred to as the "Lion of Fallujah." Zembiec graduated from the Naval Academy on May 31, 1995. He then served in the U.S. Marine Corps from 1995 until he was killed in action in 2007—serving combat tours in Kosovo, Afghanistan, and Iraq. Major Zembiec was a Force Recon officer in every sense of those words. After his death, his family found some of his writings, including the following passage under the heading, "Lessons From My Father":

> *Be a man of principle. Fight for what you believe in. Keep your word. Live with integrity. Be brave. Believe in something bigger than yourself. Serve your country. Teach. Mentor. Give something back to society. Lead from the front. Conquer your fears. Be a good friend. Be humble and be self-confident. Appreciate your friends and family. Be a leader and not a follower. Be valorous on the field of battle. And take responsibility for your actions.*

I thought about Major Zembiec's words many times during my recovery and I still think about them today. I try to apply them to my personal and to my professional lives. I think that they probably apply to everyone serving in a leadership capacity and, for that reason, I will continue to refer to these words throughout this book.

KEY TAKEAWAYS

1. When you make a command decision, act swiftly using all the intelligence at your disposal.

2. A great leader will make it a priority to take care of those around her.

3. Never, never, never give in.

Lieutenant Colonel Constantine and Corpsman George Grant together enjoying the 2014 Wounded Warrior Project annual gala.

These signs were constant reminders to us in Iraq to stay vigilant. The same is true when it comes to your personal integrity.

CHAPTER 2

PRINCIPLES AND INTEGRITY
IN THE WORKPLACE

MAJOR ZEMBIEC'S QUOTE DESCRIBES leadership, and many of the ideals he put to paper run throughout this book. I believe those principles give an individual a firm foundation to build upon, no matter their particular task in life. To begin this chapter, I want to call attention to the first lines from his quote: "Be a man of principle. Fight for what you believe in. Keep your word. Live with integrity."

Those words ring especially true for those in leadership positions in companies. To me, aspiring to these principles is the difference between building your house on a foundation of bedrock and one of sand. It does not take an architect to figure out that a house built on a firm foundation is going to weather storms better than one constructed on a beach. As individuals, we need something akin to that structural integrity at our core.

I want to point out, here, that I am talking about *your* foundation, not that of your company. Any successful business should also be built upon principles, but we are responsible for ourselves, first. Your personal foundation transcends any place you work and allows you to use your talents in any position or company you may find yourself. Your principles and your values are what you stand for, what you believe in, and what you will not compromise.

Study after study has found that companies that have high, clear, and inspiring values consistently outperform other companies in the same industry who do not. We also know that those who perform at high levels are very clear about what they believe in, and those who perform at an average level are blurred as to their beliefs. The high performers will not compromise their values and principles; others will compromise for even the slightest advantage.

So here are the questions: What are your values? What do you stand for? Most importantly, if you ask other people around you, would they say that your values are evident in how you deal with others?

If you own the company, no matter what its size, your principles are most likely the guiding force for the business. You may have a handful of employees and you may have to wear many hats. You may have to be HR, have to do marketing, or have to run to Staples, etc. The bigger you get, though, the more you will have to delegate various company operations—it would be impossible to get anything done otherwise. Good solid principles that your employees can relate to and respect will guide the company to a certain degree of success as you grow. Having guiding principles in place will help the company to survive economic fluctuations and the uncertainties of the marketplace that always seem to crop up. Operating your company from a foundation of honesty and being known for keeping your word will go a long way to securing long-term customers. In a small company owned by one individual, that person's principles are there for everyone to see—and to judge. The buck truly stops with the owner.

In larger companies, the lines between the person at the very top and the rest of the management team can get a little fuzzy to say the least. The bigger the organization, the more complex the operations become. A *good* owner or CEO should have a solid core of values to guide the running of her entire business. An *excellent* CEO or owner, though, should make sure that his managers and employees are trained in those values and that they conduct their responsibilities accordingly. In an ideal world, that is just what happens: the CEO or owner has certain values that he translates into his managers who, in turn, translate those values to the employees. In short, in an ideal world, everyone operates from the same beliefs.

Sadly, though, that is not always the case. Depending on where you happen to be in the company's hierarchy, various forces may be pulling and pushing you in ways that you do not like. Your company may have a great set of principles it operates on, but you may answer to someone who plays a bit fast and loose with those principles. In fact, you should reflect from time to time in your own career upon your own integrity and adherence to principles.

Integrity in the Marine Corps means an uprightness of character and soundness of moral principles. As we often say, having integrity means doing the right thing, even when no one is looking. It encompasses the qualities of truthfulness and honesty. A Marine's word is her bond. For Marines, nothing less than complete honesty in all their dealings—with subordinates, peers, and superiors alike—is acceptable. As I have heard retired Chairman of the Joint Chiefs of Staff General Peter Pace say on several occasions, "If you have integrity, nothing else matters. If you don't have integrity, nothing else matters."

No matter what you do, from working the streets of Fallujah to working the boardroom in New York, you should approach whatever you do at work with a long-range attitude, a focus on the future and on grand goals. This applies whether you view your current company as a place where you want to be for quite some time or you view it as important to do a good job in a present, stepping-stone, position for your larger career. Many of you readers may be contract managers for a very specific time frame and purpose. In that case, you may know that you will be moving on after the assignment is finished. Especially then, you will want to follow-through and follow-through well so that you receive a great recommendation from the company or inspire them to consider you for a permanent position. Regardless, you want the people you work for and with to know you are a person of integrity. There is nothing more valuable in this day and age than a person who accomplishes what he says he will.

That is one of the foundations of the Marine Corps—to continually strive for mission accomplishment. If I told my commanding officer what I was going to achieve in any given week in Iraq, I was going to move heaven and earth to do it. We may not always achieve 100% success, but my superiors would know that the actions my team and I took were taken in wholehearted pursuit of our goals. No matter the obstacles we encountered or the successes we won, we always learned from everything we went through so that we could do it better the next time.

While it is vitally important that your supervisors know they can trust you, it is just as important—and perhaps more important—for those who answer to you to know you are a person of integrity. Whatever the particulars of your job, you are in a management position because someone trusts that you can handle having a team of people under you. We will go into this more in another chapter, but, in brief, as a manager, you are responsible for those people who work for you.

Sometimes, I think the lack of attention to that simple fact is the single biggest mistake corporate America makes today. Everyone gets uptight about pleasing her bosses and focuses their attention solely in that direction—upward in the hierarchy. There is nothing wrong with focusing on a boss's affections, but too often, it comes at the expense of hurting those very people a manager is responsible for, those doing so much of the actual, useful, productive work of an organization.

Think for a minute how an environment valuing integrity could foster a better atmosphere at work. If you are a manager, it all starts with your integrity: sticking to your principles. You cannot be responsible for how a person above you performs. However, you are responsible for how you perform your own job. That is what your immediate subordinates will see and react to. The best way to make sure that you are going to be a success is to make sure that your team is a success. That *is* something you can control. And that is the essence of good management.

While sticking to your principles is honorable (a word that has, unfortunately, gone out of fashion in some corporations), it also gives the people who report to you an example of something that is hard to value and harder to come by: consistency. One of the hardest things to do is to work for someone when you do not know what they expect of you from day to day. We know that one of the things that is necessary for an employee to meet their supervisor's expectations is to understand clearly what those expectations are. Therefore, a principle that should guide you as a manager is to make sure you effectively communicate those expectations and *be consistent* in how you judge your employees' actions against those expectations.

Having integrity of your own principles helps breed a consistent pattern of performance for your employees. That consistency means that your employees will know what they are going to encounter when they come to work. If you, the supervisor are a "friend" one day and belittling them as "boss" in front of colleagues the next, then you are going to have a jittery employee. It cannot be fun coming to work when you do not know what boss you are going to have that day. Is today going to bring the second coming of Attila the Hun or a church pastor? A healthy work environment is not one where your workers are walking around on eggshells until they determine your temperament for the day. It may take a little effort and practice, but if you present a stable persona to your subordinates, it is going to be a great deal easier for them to work with you. Likewise, if employees aren't afraid of the boss shooting the messenger, they will be more likely to come to you if there is a problem that needs addressed. Too many issues spiral out of control at work simply because people are afraid to go to their supervisor when something goes a bit wrong. It is much more productive to solve a problem early than it is to hide it.

One of the most wonderful things that I took from my time in the Marines—and carry and cherish and preach to this day—is the constant training toward maintaining our integrity and adhering to principles. I realized that our leaders did not mean those should be our guiding principles only when we were on duty. Rather, they wanted those principles to be something we carried with us for the rest of our lives. They taught us that being a "Marine" was not something that only happened when we wore the uniform. It was to be part of our very being. It is often said, among us in the know at least, that "there is no such thing as an ex-Marine." It is because we train in principles that that statement is so true.

Likewise, constantly exercising your integrity at work is going to carry over into all aspects of your own life. Do you know how important and great that is? Say you are a parent. Your integrity is a quality that your kids are going to see in everything you do and, therefore, it is something they are more likely to learn themselves. The same is true of your spouse or significant other. When it comes to parenting or relationships, trust and consistency are so important that they often determine the difference between smooth sailing and a force 10 storm. When those closest to you know they can depend upon you, it makes for a much happier life.

True integrity does not have an on and off switch. Of course, none of us are perfect and there are going to be times or situations where we do not follow through as much as we would have liked to. However, you need to aim to maintain your integrity as consistently as possible. As a supervisor, if they know you have integrity, then your best people will be much, much more willing to work for you. The people you report to will see that success and reward you accordingly. Most corporations want to promote people who do good work, maintain a positive attitude, and inspire their teams to improve their capabilities. So, although it may take time, keep on a steady and honorable course at work and that will pay huge dividends.

You will also find, in the end, that integrity will keep your department, or the entire company, on a steady and successful heading. If you are in a top position at your company, one that guides the entire business, then you need to get everyone on the same page regarding your principles. You need your staff to have that same vision and to desire to function with the same degree of integrity as you. There is a lot to be gained from having diverse team members. But not on foundational principles. Everyone needs to hold true to principles like honesty and respect or the team's trust will be lacking, either from team members to management or between team members. In either case, that hurts the chances for success. This principle also applies if you are in charge of a small department. Everybody needs to be rowing in the same direction or you will be going around in circles.

Did you know that exploration hundreds of years ago plateaued until the compass was invented? Navigation could only go so far using the sun and stars. When the compass came along, sailors could, for the first time, venture far away from land and keep on a steady course. They were also able to get back home. Your integrity and moral compass perform the same function in the workplace. You know where you want to go and how to get there. If something comes up that knocks you off course, you can fall back on your moral compass to reestablish your direction.

In the Marine Corps, you can have a perfect battle plan on paper. However, battles are never perfect. In fact, we often say that even the best plans do not survive first contact with the enemy. Things happen that you did not or even could not have prepared for, just out of the blue, which change the immediate actions in the field, but the objective remains the same. I did not expect to get shot that October day, but the Marines around me were trained for such an event and they performed their tasks very well. To put it mildly, something came up and my Marines responded—beautifully.

Business operates in the same way. Changing economic conditions, the loss of a key customer, an industry you depend upon going on strike, or any number of other disruptions can drastically alter how you must do business. If your company operates from core principles, however, then management can fall back on them to maneuver in a different direction without losing focus on where the organization needs to go.

There is a reason why successful athletes practice their sport hour after hour for days on end. A body develops muscle memory. That helps the athlete perform well even if conditions are not perfect. Constantly sticking to and practicing our principles allows us to do the same thing at work. Whatever the situation or crisis, we can continue to plow ahead in the right direction.

By having a firm set of principles, we also do well when we face indecision. Situations arise where you do not have as much information as you would like. In fact, rarely do we have all the information we would like, let alone all the information we need. This is often the case in battle, and this is often the case in civilian life, both in and out of work. When indecision occurs, you can fall back on your principles to help make the decision. If you have good solid principles and apply them to the issue, chances are that you will be able to successfully address the problem. Maintaining your integrity and your principles will make the difference between coming up with a "guess" and an "educated guess" to solve a problem.

Remember how I mentioned earlier that the word "honorable" seems out of vogue in business these days? It was not always that way. Leaders in business cemented many important deals over the years with just a handshake. In many cases, a business owner's word was as good as a contract. Today, despite the word of a businessman and sometimes despite the contract, as well, small advantages are often taken in pursuit of one more dollar.

There is no reason, however, that we cannot be honorable in our own little spheres of influence. True, we must be wary of those we deal with in today's culture, but we will reap huge gains if we let our employees know they can depend on what we say. Keeping your word will only make you more successful in the long run, no matter what you undertake in work or life. That simple practice may be the highest degree of integrity any of us can exercise. If we do that one thing, it gives credibility and validity to all of the other principles we want to enact at work.

Consider this: On November 10, 1775, at a bar called Tun Tavern in Philadelphia, two battalions of Continental Marines were formed as an infantry force capable of fighting for independence both at sea and on shore. The formal United States Marine Corps was born on July 11, 1798. For over two hundred years, the Marines have defended and fought for our country. The integrity and principles displayed by Corps' members allowed them to thrive over the other services of that time. Now, that is a success story you want to emulate in your role in your company!

Take the first step today. It is a good idea to actually write down your principles for both work and for life in general. I hope that they are the same for both. Writing your principles down makes them real, concrete, and something you can refer back to when things get tough. Keep in mind that your list of principles is always a work in progress. However, if you have the integrity to stick to your principles, that will be your key to succeed in business over the long run.

KEY TAKEAWAYS

1. Cherishing integrity and acting consistently is a great combination.

2. Having solid core principles is critical to personal and professional success.

3. Honorable actions are contagious—inspire others around you by doing the right thing.

Just as it is important to continually practice with your various weapons systems to maintain proficiency, the same is true for practicing your principles.

It is all about the team. Our small team here is in front of our warehouse, which quickly became our new home in Iraq.

CHAPTER 3

WHY YOUR VISION MATTERS

WINSTON CHURCHILL SAID, "THE empires of the future are empires of the mind." Like many successful military and business leaders throughout the ages, Churchill knew that every desired goal starts with an exciting vision. True leaders project into the future and imagine what that ideal future will look like. A big question a good leader should constantly ask is, "How do we get where we want to go from where we are today?"

As a leader, it is important to develop your vision. It does not matter if you are a corporate CEO, a mid-level manager, or just starting your first business. This process begins with being able to clearly articulate your vision and the steps needed to achieve it. Those steps mean setting realistic, demanding goals, and then going after them relentlessly. A wise leader understands this to mean that he has to have the help of other talented men and women who are equally committed and engaged.

Great leaders spend time identifying the values and ideas they are most passionate about fulfilling. Contrary to popular thought, securing money or prestige is not what drives most successful people. Rather, money and prestige are a byproduct of the process—granted, a very nice byproduct—that comes out of the quest to realize the vision.

Henry Ford visualized a car that every family could afford. Steve Jobs dreamed of putting a computer in the hands of everyday people. General Dwight Eisenhower envisioned using not only military strength but also economic aid, diplomacy, and information to stabilize fragile nations, a concept that is particularly important 70 years later. What is your vision? What are the steps you have to take to get there?

My vision for our team heading to Iraq was that we would be as physically and mentally prepared as possible and that we would all know our jobs inside and out. I wanted our team to attach seamlessly to the infantry battalion, be a true resource for Lieutenant Colonel Desgrosseilliers, and to all come home safely. Our mobilization orders started on June 15, 2006, and we had just over two months to train before we deployed to Iraq. We coordinated our efforts with the other teams in our detachment and trained very hard every day toward our goal. A typical day included physical training, weapons training, situational walk-throughs (so we would be prepared for our field exercises), and various classes related to Iraqi culture, civil affairs, and the Marine Corps planning process. My good friend Jason Brezler, a fantastic leader and one of the other team leaders in our detachment, came up with the idea of having each of our Marines read a book related to our mission in some broad way. Each was then to give a report about the lessons that she learned from the book to our unit. Each of these activities, from physical training to the book report, tied into my vision that we would be as ready as possible. I relied heavily on my fellow Team Leaders, but also on each member of my own team.

To develop your mission, but especially to communicate it with clarity, it is vital to ensure that you can succinctly identify what the mission is. Succinct and clear identification of the mission will make it much more likely that others will buy into it. It is that individual and group buy-in that will motivate the entire team to move forward to accomplish the mission. This is true for a captain on a battlefield, a manager at a team meeting, or a politician launching a new campaign.

The Marines have a unique mission statement among the branches of the U.S. Armed Forces: They "shall, at any time, be liable to do duty in the forts and garrisons of the United States, on the seacoast, or any other duty on shore, as the president, at his discretion, shall direct."

Wherever the commander in chief wants us, we go. All of the energies of the Marines center on the training of its leaders and members to be as ready as possible to fulfill that mission. Today, that overall mission may take on a hundred different forms at any one time anywhere in the world, but the Marines never waver from the ultimate vision.

That same mentality is and should be present in business. A company's focus may be on producing a particular type of product or service, but a good business will look to do more than that—thinking to the future and planning for tomorrow is the only way to stay competitive. To demonstrate this, let us look at one of America's biggest companies. The mission statement of Google is pretty much the same mission as any Internet search engine company: *"Google's mission is to organize the world's information and make it universally accessible and useful."*

The unofficial mission statement for Google, though, gives more insight into the company's vision. It was included in the company's 2004 IPO prospectus and was backed up by the explanation that "We believe strongly that in the long term, we will be better served—as shareholders and in all other ways—by a company that does good things for the world even if we forgo some short term gains." That unofficial mission statement of Google is *"Don't Be Evil."*

Their vision is a little more than helping you find stuff on the Internet, right?

Now many of you may be saying, "I am only a small cog in this behemoth company. How is my vision going to matter?"

It is going to matter to the people with whom you work. It is going to be a huge deal to the folks who report to you. And, if you effectively communicate your vision to your team, providing a consistent goal, then it will most likely show to your superiors, making this a huge deal to those to whom you report as well. I was just one officer out of almost 200,000 other Marines, but I made a difference to my team of Marines in the same way that you can make a difference with your team. Imagine that your company is a huge hotel in New York City. In that hotel, your little department may only be one small suite among hundreds. It is not the size, but rather your vision that will ultimately affect how well your little piece of the real estate functions. Yes, you have to perform to the specifics of your job description, but how you go about that performance is going to be up to you. Having a good vision of what is important to you and your team and of how you want to conduct business will set you up for long-term success.

Your vision will not come to you in a flash of brilliance or in a vacuum. It is common knowledge that an organization's single biggest asset is its people. To define your vision realistically, you have to understand what drives your people, what their values are, and what they are capable of accomplishing with the right support and direction. You also need to have an intimate understanding of your corporate culture and the key characteristics of your business environment.

Implementing and fulfilling your vision will take more than simply identifying it, though. All successful leaders take action and constantly drive their people and teams toward their vision. Once you identify the necessary steps you need to take and the resources you need to commit to achieve your vision—do it! Implement! Leaders must always move forward, face danger and uncertainty, and take risks when there is no guarantee of success. Great leaders know that, most often, the greatest danger is to do nothing in a world that is changing very rapidly. Young military officers are encouraged to take bold, decisive action, and the same holds true for young people with ambition in the business context. When you fail to constantly move toward your vision, you let others shape your destiny. Even when you fail, the best course of action is to move forward, learn from the failure, assess the repercussions of your actions, and implement what you learned for a better result next time. As they say in the military, the imperfect plan violently executed today is always better than a perfect plan executed two weeks from now.

In fact, we have a lot to learn from our failures as we push toward our vision. Thomas Edison and his researchers, for example, had been trying to develop a nickel-iron battery for more than five months when a friend visited him in his laboratory. The story goes that a friend learned that Edison had made over 9,000 experiments in trying to devise this new type of storage battery, but that he had not produced a single thing that promised to solve the question. Seeing the immense amount of thought and labor that his friend had expended, fruitlessly, he thought, the friend asked, "Isn't it a shame that with the tremendous amount of work you have done, you haven't been able to get any results?" Edison replied, "Results! Why, man, I have gotten a lot of results! I know several thousand things that won't work!"

Brian Tracy, a leadership and personal development expert, teaches us that a helpful exercise in developing and articulating your vision is to imagine five years have passed and that your organization is perfect in every respect. You have the highest recognized product or service in the market, high levels of sales and profitability, the best people, the best operations, and the best technology. What would your company look like, perfected, in five years if this were all true? Take that and identify how you can get there from where you are today. Ascertain what you have to do to be recognized by the market as the best in your business, what core competencies you need to achieve that goal, and how you train your people in those competencies.

That vision for achieving perfection should not be a secret agenda. Let everyone know what your vision is and keep your staff and key players involved. Disseminate your vision far and wide. Take bold, decisive action when necessary. Synchronize your actions with your company's well-defined mission and purpose. Then, ultimately, your vision will become your reality.

Your vision naturally ties into leadership and personal responsibility. Everyone can grow to be an excellent leader, if leadership is what they want to do. Sure, there are those few individuals we have run into throughout our lives who are "natural born leaders." But they are few and far between. And even out of that select group, those who are continually successful in life are the ones who make the effort to learn how to sharpen their skills. For the most part, leaders are made, not born. Even if born with innate leadership potential, that potential takes development and honing to be most effective. So, if you want to be an excellent leader, it is just like anything else—you have to study and learn and put your time in and be seen as the guy who gets the job done.

Look at my own situation leading up to Iraq: I had never worked as part of the infantry or been directly responsible for Marines outside an office environment. But I had gone through the same training that all Marine officers go through, had implemented as much as I could in our office, had read many books about leadership, and had attended guest lectures. When the time came, I was ready.

Was I nervous knowing that I would be going to a war zone? Was I worried that I was going to be the one who was ultimately responsible for the lives of my Marines? Of course. This was especially true when I checked in with Lieutenant Colonel Desgrosseilliers in Iraq. I mentioned earlier that the wall next to his office was covered with the pictures of all the young Marines from the battalion who had been killed in action. That was sobering, to say the least, but I had confidence in myself, and I had done everything I could to be prepared. There is no secret chromosome for leadership. You have to make it a priority. Remember, being a leader does not only mean being the CEO. Just like the Marine Corps, there are many different levels of leadership within your company. Each level provides opportunities to prove yourself.

It is also incredibly important to take personal responsibility for your actions. An author named Cynthia Kersey wrote that the foundation for creating incredible results is to realize that, ultimately, we are solely responsible for the quality of our lives--period. And she's right. The moment that you realize that you hold the solution to the very challenges you face is the moment your life changes. That realization puts you in control of your life. You are free to move forward, to overcome any obstacle in your path, and to create the life you really want.

When you have a vision to aim for as a leader, and you couple that with a sense of personal responsibility, you will go far and you can bring many people along with you.

A sure sign of a company having problems is if its Human Resources department entrance is a revolving door. One of the chief complaints of most companies' leadership ranks is that there is constant turnover and they "cannot find the right people."

I challenge them to look in the mirror. To me, it sounds like they do not have the right leadership. Say you have two companies: Each hires 20 people who pretty much have the same qualities, level of experience, etc. One company tells them what their job is and tells them to get to it. Two months later, when they do not perform up to the company's standards, they get booted out the door. The company then has to hire 20 new people, and the revolving door continues to turn.

Meanwhile, the other company brings the new employees in and gives them some initial training. They are then able to start their duties. The employees are not working in a vacuum, however, as there is a strong group of leaders who watch, coach, and evaluate the employees and the process itself. In this company, if a person is let go after two months, it is because they were not really trying, even with all the help and support provided.

That may sound like an extreme example, but this stark contrast between companies is exactly what is happening in corporate America today. Bad, ineffective leadership looks at people solely as a resource to be used up, rather than nurtured. Often, it is a constant focus on the short-term needs of a company that allows this type of behavior to exist and continue. Then, at senior staff meetings, the key leadership wonders why the company never meets any of its long-term goals.

If you are a manager, the odds are pretty good that you have to answer to people above you and that you are responsible for people below you—throw in having to work with your peers, and you have quite a juggling act. However, if you are able to establish a vision for yourself as to what you want to achieve in life, then that vision will help you work in a manner where you are able to be in sync with those around you, both above and below. Your bosses will be happy and people will enjoy working with you, and so will the other managers at your level. It all comes down to how you conduct yourself and how important your integrity is to you.

As I said, understanding and articulating your vision does not happen overnight. Take the time to really think about what you want to achieve and how you want to go about it. If you work for yourself, you can make this vision the foundation of your business. If you are in a corporate structure, see how your vision dovetails with the company's goals. If your vision does not gel with the company you currently work for, it is not a crime to seek out a new company with a culture more aligned with your own. In fact, you will be better at your job when you enjoy the culture as well as the work.

Remaining focused on your vision and continuing to put forth the effort to reach it—one step at a time—is what separates life's great achievers from those who merely dream, but never act.

KEY TAKEAWAYS

1. Only by identifying a strategic vision can you really determine long-term measurable goals.

2. Leadership is a skill anyone can learn, especially with today's easy access to books, magazines, webinars, TED Talks, and other online videos.

3. Being a great leader means that you are willing to take a good hard look at yourself and honestly identify your strengths as well as your weaknesses.

It is okay to feel nervous about the risks you may encounter. This was one of our vehicles that was blown up two days before I was shot.

I was honored to be promoted to major by Lieutenant Colonel Todd Desgrosseilliers. I learned a lot about taking care of your people just by watching him in action.

CHAPTER 4

LEADING FROM THE FRONT:
LEAD, TRUST, SUPPORT, MOTIVATE

STARTING FROM WHEN I first attended Officer Candidates School almost 20 years ago, the Marine Corps consistently pounded into my head the right way to take care of those whom you have the privilege to lead. It is a sacred responsibility to lead people in any environment, on the battlefield or in the business world.

There are three general schools of thought that a person in a management position follows. The first follows the idea that you have a responsibility to those under you (like in the Marines). The second is that those who report to you are pawns for your use in meeting your goals. The third is where you simply do not give much thought to your position as a manager of others. How your thinking is shaped comes from your mentors, corporate culture, experience, and training—or the lack thereof. Personally, I believe that the only way to be a good leader of other men and women is to realize that those under you are your responsibility. You are there to make them effective in their own jobs, to be a true resource for them, and to empower them to operate at their highest potential. The great byproduct of this approach is that, before you know it, you have met your personal and professional goals, and your company is successful and profitable.

If that is the best way to run a department, or even an entire company, then why are there so many managers who fall into one of the last two schools of thought? Many times, that is because the person does not know any better. Managerial philosophy is simply not an integral part of a company's way of doing business or its training initiatives. In such a company, a manager is not going to have the necessary tools to get good at his job. Many managers and supervisors are promoted into their positions because they did a great job at a lower level. But they often have received no leadership training to help them expand their focus and scope of influence. Focusing on these new leaders is critical for a company's success.

Very often, an employee is elevated to her first management position without any prior leadership experience. Jane or John Doe may have been very good at making widgets, so the company suddenly promotes them to managing a small section of the operation. Unless the company provides training, they are not going to know what it means to lead. Unfortunately, if they had a manager who operated by yelling and threatening, this is the example they are going to take with them onto the factory floor. This occurs all too often in any type of business or organization. Another good example is when a great salesperson is made into a sales manager. That person may have no idea how to motivate others to be good at sales. And, in fact, the company may be hurt twice: Not only do they now have an ineffective leader of salespeople, but they have also lost one of their best sellers!

A person can only operate based on what they know. This is a basic tenet. Too many times, new parents model their behavior on how their parents raised them. If their parents were terrible, then the newest generation is going to face the same pitfalls. However, more enlightened people will realize that how they were brought up may have left a lot to be desired. Those parents will actively strive to learn how to be better parents for their children. This may mean reading, research, talking to a parent they admire, etc. Business works the same way. As mentioned in the previous chapter, a "born" leader is a rare thing. Companies and individuals can take steps to mold their managers to lead according to a process better than "that's how my boss did it."

Just like in the Marine Corps, I believe the number one concept that a leader at any level needs to take to heart is that he has a responsibility to those under him. Once you learn this and, more importantly, live it at work, then it becomes a part of you. In today's business climate, where it is easy for your most highly qualified employees to find new job opportunities, a big difference in keeping them engaged as part of your team—and, therefore, more likely to stay—comes down to how they are treated. Constant communication means that employees always know about work conditions in other offices, and there is a growing understanding that employees are no longer motivated simply by money. No, taking care of your people has to be your number one priority.

In any discussion about leadership, we have to start with the premise that it is not just about effective management, but that a great leader puts his employees' needs first and empowers them to perform at their highest levels. It is great to have lofty goals and great expectations for people who report to you. However, if those employees do not feel that the objectives are attainable or that you will not do all you can to help them achieve them, then they will experience a great deal of frustration. When that happens on a prolonged basis, frustration turns into counter-productivity.

When I was in Iraq, I made it a priority to lead our team on every night mission, every patrol, and in every aspect of our training. I also pushed some of that responsibility down to the lower levels of my command to help develop others as leaders, too. However, I would never ask any of my Marines to do something that I was not willing to do.

In my summers during college, I worked for Fairfax City, Virginia, on an asphalt crew paving roads and conducting other repairs. I learned that when the city manager had first started working there, he spent a whole day on the back end of a trash truck. That was not easy work for him, but he wanted to experience a day in the lives of some of his employees so he could better understand their perspective.

That idea is especially valuable in other industries, and in your operating space, no doubt. You cannot expect the supervisors below you to properly learn all they need to know about working with their people if you yourself are not willing to practice "management by walking around" and showing genuine interest in your people. Getting your hands dirty and "walking the walk" will truly affect your team's loyalty, which will affect every aspect of their performance, including their customer service, from which higher profits will naturally follow. Despite our differences in rank and responsibility, I often worked side by side with my Marines, even if the task was something mundane such as cleaning a warehouse. By doing so, I developed a deep camaraderie with my team, based primarily on spending time together and demonstrating my commitment to them.

Your concern and interest in your employees has to be real. In 1980, the comedian George Burns published a memoir titled, "The Third Time Around." In that memoir, he included a chapter about his late-blooming career in motion pictures. He offered the following advice to young performers: *"And remember this for the rest of your life: To be a fine actor, when you're playing a role, you've got to be honest. And if you can fake that, you've got it made."* That works in the movies. That works on the television screen. That does not work in real life. If you cannot muster up true empathy and pride for the people who report to you, then you are not going to go as far as you think you should in your company. It may even be time to consider another position or occupation.

When it comes to customer service, you cannot expect your employees to treat each customer with the highest level of respect if you do not do the same thing for them. Many companies provide the same or similar products and services. Unless your price is so much less for the same quality of goods than the price at another company, the only place you can really distinguish your business is in customer service. If a customer perceives bad treatment from the company he is buying from, then he is going to look for a company where he can have a better experience and will spend his money there instead. If a manager spends a meeting yelling and cursing at his staff, they are not going to be smiling on the phone when they talk to a customer. I am not talking about one bad day here or there. I am talking about where the work environment or command climate is consistently negative and contentious. Like it or not, that is what is going to filter down to the customer. So do not start the attitude and do not allow that attitude.

In a military engagement, a group of Marines is going to respond better when they have the utmost confidence and respect for their leader. That is what I saw from my leaders in the Marine Corps, and that is how I wanted others to perceive me, too. I am alive and writing today because this style of leadership meant that everyone I came into contact with immediately after I was shot did their job to the best of their ability. Corpsman George Grant reacted from training, without thought to his own life. Lieutenant Colonel Desgrosseilliers's command decisions were immediate and saved my life. Drs. Bilski, Christopher, and Blankenship each reacted immediately—after some shock over hearing that a JAG officer had been shot through the head (Dr. Bilski recalled saying aloud, *"Are you kidding me?!"*)—and perfectly to stop my incredible bleeding and prep me for the helo ride to Balad. That series of perfect, synchronized actions does not happen by accident. It comes from example, from training, and from a conscientious effort to have each individual want to do the best they can, no matter the situation they may be thrown into. Lieutenant Colonel Desgrosseilliers's reaction was not only incredible, but displayed the true spirit of leading from the front and taking care of those around you. But more about that in chapter 6.

You cannot expect your staff to live and breathe your vision for your team unless you live and breathe that vision yourself. You must effectively communicate that vision to them through many different channels. We viewed leading Marines as a privilege—not a right or just some other job—and it is a privilege you have to earn every day. The same is true in the workplace. Working with others carries the same challenges in any relationship. It is a matter of respect and communication. You have to respect those who report to you as individuals, and you cannot take them for granted. They are not pawns on a chessboard, but people, complex and deep. For most employees, if you are fair with them and let them know what is going on and why, many of them will run through brick walls for you. It is not because you screamed and ordered them to, but because they want to do it.

Leadership is not only having the proper knowledge of how to lead people, but the right attitude in doing it. There is a story about a stranger who is approaching the outskirts of a town. An old man is sitting on a chair in front of his house and asks the stranger why he is coming into town. The stranger says, "I got tired of where I was living. The people were mean-spirited. They were always gossiping and picking fights. Nothing ever went right and nobody liked each other. I had to get out of there and thought I would try this place."

The old man said, "Just as you found things there, so you will find here."

A couple hours later, another stranger approached town and the old man asked the same question. This stranger replied, "I come from a place that was terrific. It seemed like the sun was always out, even on a stormy day. Everybody got along, and worked and played together. I wanted to explore the rest of the area so I wanted to come spend some time here."

The old man said, "Just as you found things there, so you will find here."

As the story illustrates, how we think and act is going to affect the environment we are in. A manager is the driving force in determining how her employees will think of their work. If you are a manager, you set the atmosphere of the workplace. It is your leadership and your example that sets the stage for success or failure. To some people, this may sound like an awesome bit of responsibility. And you know what? It is! There are not too many better feelings in the world than knowing that you led others to be successful, and that those people would do anything for you.

Leadership starts from the top. At this point in my life, I have talked with many mid-level managers who did not exactly have great examples to learn from in those above them. While that is surely a shame, I counsel them that they can be the ones to break the negative leadership model in their company. They can be the change they want to see. Just like the parent who does not want to repeat the bad parenting they had, any manager can decide to set a better example than that set for them to date. Remember, success breeds imitation. If your department shows significant progress, then the company is going to ask you what you are doing differently. The company may then start to adapt your lessons for the rest of the organization—giving you another nice byproduct, pretty good stock with others in the company.

Corporate America is all over the map with the strengths of leadership demonstrated in its companies, big and small alike. It runs the gauntlet from poor to mediocre to great, and includes everything in between. It is not necessarily the profit margin that distinguishes great leadership from poor. Some companies are so huge or so well placed that they can make money in spite of their leadership shortcomings. It is only by looking at the many intangibles that also compose a company that we can identify the effectiveness of its leadership style.

A good example of leadership style positively affecting operations was highlighted for me on a recent trip I took with James Schenck, CEO of Pentagon Federal Credit Union, to a couple of their call centers in Omaha, Nebraska. Perhaps that does not sound like the beginning to a glamorous trip, but I learned a lot while I was there. I discovered a lot about James's leadership style and human nature, generally.

PenFed has 1,500 employees, and we had the opportunity to talk with 400 of them while we were in Omaha. I think if more companies or government agencies did what James did, employees would be much happier in the workplace and feel more connected at work. As I told James, due to the nature of my business, I have worked with many corporations over the last couple of years. It is rare, in my experience, to see a CEO have such personal interaction with his employees.

I knew things were going to go well as soon as we arrived: James either knew the employees at the front door or immediately introduced himself to them and quickly found out what they did there. He obviously was very comfortable walking through the various workspaces, and he spent a significant amount of time answering questions, identifying priorities, and, perhaps most importantly, listening.

I visited both of their call centers to provide a keynote presentation about teamwork, overcoming adversity, and the upside of change. The presentations went quite well and it moved me to see how many of the staff lined up afterward to talk with me, tell me about their military service or that of a loved one, or just to show their support to the veteran and wounded warrior communities. I am always heartened by how the country supports those who have been in the military. The attitude in these offices was clearly a positive one and it showed in how I was treated.

Before I spoke, James updated everyone in the room about the new policies at PenFed, his team's priorities for the coming year, and their expansion goals. However, he also took the time to address a number of questions that employees had emailed to him, and to answer those questions that members of the audience had at the time. Outside of the military, I have rarely seen a CEO do something like that. James and the rest of the leadership of PenFed regularly do this in the course of their work. I could see how happy the staff was to have a chance to talk with their CEO in person and address a wide variety of issues.

It was especially interesting to me to see how many of the staff's questions and concerns resulted in policy updates. Most great ideas about innovation and corporate growth come from employees, and that certainly played out in front of my eyes. Being an effective leader requires staying in touch with those people who support you every day by operating on the ground, and that is exactly what James did. Just like in the military, often the most productive leaders are those who spend significant time among their troops. This concept applies from the smallest start-up to the largest corporation, because engaged people truly are your most valuable asset. And the best way to engage your people is to take the time to develop relationships with, talk to, and really listen to them. I encourage other leaders to take this lesson to heart.

Management and leadership is not hiding behind your desk and a closed office door while handing out orders for your employees to follow in emailed memos. It is about knowing your people and getting their feedback on what is and is not working. Leadership is being responsive to the needs of those who follow you, and putting them in the best position to be successful in their jobs.

I heard of a situation that happened to a director in a large non-profit organization. When things were going badly with his staff and volunteers, he developed a siege mentality. He never left the office or went out to deal and talk directly with those people for whom he was responsible. The short and very sad version of this story is that it was not long before the board fired him. In military jargon, he was relieved of his command.

Most people in leadership have aspirations to higher office, to bear more responsibility. They want to be better leaders. They work at it, make mistakes and learn from them, and keep moving forward. They are rewarded with promotions and the chance to exercise their skills in some greater leadership role. This is how officers approach life in the Marines and every branch of the military. This is also true of business, government, and almost any type of organization, really.

The most successful leaders know that they do not achieve their promotions in a vacuum. They are successful because they took seriously their position and responsibility as a leader, and they knew that that meant responsibility for and to those under them. Great leaders know they are at the top of a pyramid and that they can only be there with everyone's support from beneath them. They know they depend upon those working together under them. Furthermore, they know it is a component of great leadership to get the people working for them to be successful in the performance of their own jobs. It is only in this way that they will have a firm foundation under them to showcase their leadership skills. After all, a pyramid is going to crumble if everything from the bottom to the top is not well constructed.

KEY TAKEAWAYS

1. No matter at what level, every leader has a significant responsibility for those below him.

2. You cannot lead everybody the same way and realistically expect the same results—you often have to paint with a fine stroke, not a broad brush.

3. The most productive leaders are often those who regularly engage with their employees.

Major Constantine with Sergeant Howard. By working closely with this stellar non-commissioned officer, I learned that I could trust him implicitly.

Semper Fidelis means Always Faithful, and for Marines our motto emphasizes a complete commitment to the mission.

CHAPTER 5

PUTTING YOUR PEOPLE FIRST

THE TITLE OF THIS chapter may be a foreign concept to many people. Today we are surrounded by social media where people can put up virtually unlimited photos, comments, and videos that shout "look at me" to the world. HR managers tell you about prospective employees coming to interviews who focus, aloud, not on "this is how I can help your company," but rather, "what is in this job for me?" In this environment, especially, you sometimes see executives who are completely oblivious to the needs and concerns of their subordinates. And those execs wonder why there is such a disconnect throughout the company!

As opposed to that, think about the motto of the Marine Corps – Semper Fi. It means "always faithful," and it reflects a mindset shared by all Marines.

Think about how powerful those two words are: It is not just "sometimes faithful" or "faithful when it is convenient." It is a complete commitment to the mission. It is a two-way street that runs up and down the entire organization. For us, Semper Fi means putting your life on the line for the Marine to your left, for the Marine to your right, the one out front, and the one behind.

I will show you some hard examples of this in a moment, but first I want to focus on the "two-way street" idea just expressed. Truly and consistently excellent companies do not function on a dictatorial basis. In other words, while final decisions are the responsibility of the people at the top of the hierarchical ladder, these leaders arrive at their conclusions only after listening to and evaluating the ideas of the people doing the actual work. Marine leaders will base their decisions on the best information they have available in a given situation. If the matter at hand is a battle, intelligence is paramount to accomplishing the mission with minimal casualties. The same should be true when a manager, at any level, faces a decision. Often the best feedback you are going to receive is from those under you.

Being a good leader depends on many different qualities. In the corporate world, decisiveness, confidence, clarity of communication, and mission accomplishment are commonly cited as strengths. They certainly are good examples, but the one quality that should wrap the entire leadership package and top it in a bow is wisdom. In leadership, the manager's ability to comprehend that her employees are her most important resource, is the key to that wisdom. A manager's mindset cannot be, "I don't need these people to be successful." That leader needs to have the wisdom to say, "I cannot do this without them." While some turnover will occur in any organization, a manager must realize that he needs these people for their strengths and loyalty, not just that he needs X number of employees to accomplish some end.

Always faithful in the workplace means the manager can depend on the employee and the employee can depend on the manager. Whatever position a person holds in a company, she wants to feel like the people above and below them have her back. It becomes impossible to excel at your job if you are constantly concerned that others that you depend upon are not doing their jobs. This encompasses every level of the organization, extending from a superior not giving you proper credit when credit is due to one of your people not actually having accomplished a task reported as having been completed.

In any business, there are plenty of situations where someone can fall down on the job, thus affecting your own work. This is going to happen, sometimes by accident or human error. However, if you take the steps of forming a trusting relationship with those you work with, that relationship and interconnectedness will minimalize potential problems resulting from any mishaps. You may be limited in what you can do to foster better working relationships with those above you, but you have full control of your end of your relationships with those who report to you.

I have seen some executives sneer at any training that promotes what they call the "touchy-feely" lessons of management. I knew one such person who took great pride in the plaque his employees gave him when he left the company. It had a nutcracker mounted to it because that is pretty much how he pushed people to get things done. I have a feeling that his department did not give him that plaque because they were sorry to see him go. After all, his department had the highest turnover rate of personnel in the entire company. His Human Resources department spent a disproportionate amount of money bringing new employees into his area, and he had become a thorn in the side of the CEO for that and other reasons. The company actually gave him a "golden parachute" deal to get him out and to repair the damage he caused within the organization and, because his actions affected the work of others, with the clients of the organization.

Leadership and management are about relationships with people. "Touchy-feely" is a negative connotation aimed at good lessons where a person learns how to properly motivate and lead his or her staff. When a leader does all of this the right way, it fosters loyalty. When you are a leader and when your people are loyal to you and to each other, you can accomplish almost anything. You will all have to work through good times and bad. Semper Fi, or always faithful, is what will bind your staff through thick and thin. In Iraq, Lieutenant Colonel Desgrosseilliers's Marines would have followed him anywhere and in fact did just that. Was that just because he outranked them? Definitely not. We all knew that he cared incredibly deeply for us, that he always led from the front, and that while his primary focus was mission accomplishment, our welfare was a close second. We all knew that before October 18, 2006. His actions that day only concreted our belief in his focus on our welfare—Semper Fi.

In the Marines, our training emphasized the importance of the team's and each individual's welfare in everything we did. It would not always be in your face, but it was there. Usually, it was conveyed by simply observing how a leader conducted himself with those under him. Whatever the rank, a leader in the Marine Corps would make an honest effort to get to know the people under her. They would be careful to set a proper example for their people. This carried more weight than all of the training in the world. You can teach people all you want about how to conduct themselves, but if the leader does not live it, then the training will have been a waste of time.

You cannot put a dollar value on loyalty. Whether you are in the military or in the business world, there are going to be times when you need to ask your people to do some things that are out of their comfort zone. If they are loyal and have confidence in you, then they will do their best to do what you ask. As a leader, this is the optimal environment you want to encourage and reinforce.

In the Marine Corps, we have a group of core concepts that we really focus on when it comes to leadership. I can summarize the most important of those concepts in just three words, just three words that, if put into practice, will create a great working environment for your employees:

Officers Eat Last

Marine leaders prioritize the accomplishment of the mission first, the welfare of their Marines second, and their own personal needs third. When meals are served, the lowest-ranking enlisted Marines eat first, and the highest-ranking officers eat last, so that each level of leadership ensures that their charges are fed first. Now, why would we do that?

When Marines see their leaders placing their group's needs before their own, they feel compelled to do the same for those around them. Perhaps more importantly, a leader's ability to convince his Marines—

through his actions, not just his words—that he truly cares for them will foster a fierce loyalty and unwavering willingness to follow. In Iraq, when I knew we would be going on a long patrol that day (and this is really just a tiny example of what others did to such a huge extent), I would ensure that we had extra Gatorade and a cooler of ice in the vehicle. Those drinks were for the Marines, and if anything was left over, that was for me. My Marines knew that, and I never went thirsty. That small act was seen by my Marines and was reciprocated through their loyalty to me and to the mission of our unit.

I can still remember our platoon sergeant (he is probably the corporate equivalent of a mid-level manager) at Officer Candidates School telling me that I would never know my troops as well as he did, but that that did not diminish my responsibility toward them in the least. By the time we got to Iraq, though, I had learned every last detail about my Marines that I could. I knew their hometowns, levels of education, family situations, job preferences, strengths, weaknesses, religious views, and political leanings. I would have to trust them with my life, and I wanted them to know our mission and their safety were my only priorities.

Leading by example is a core component of building that mindset and taking care of your people. It should be easy to understand that nobody will follow you if they do not feel that you are willing to make the same sacrifice that you are asking of them. There were times in Iraq where this meant coming back from meetings at 10:30 at night and, instead of going to sleep after an exhausting day of combat patrols, sitting up with one of my Marines to help him with his intelligence report or other administrative duties. I also know that my Marines worked incredibly hard to accomplish a wide variety of missions, because none of them wanted to feel like they had let any of the others down and not carried his own weight.

There are generally two attitudes when someone receives a promotion. One, "I don't have to work as hard as I used to." The second, and correct attitude, "I have more responsibility and more people relying on me. This is actually going to require more work in order to be successful." By understanding that this means going that extra mile for your people, you will find that they will take that extra step for you, too.

Think of your position in your company. This is exactly what you want from your staff. You can constantly tell them that you need their loyalty and have them take every training course available, but if they do not see this concept backed up by your loyalty to them, it is not going to happen. It is not as if you have to manufacture opportunities during the workday to show you care about your people and that you support them. Those opportunities occur naturally and are almost constantly present—we just have to recognize them and take advantage.

I think, first and foremost, that you have to show that you are interested in your employees. This is going to take on different dimensions depending on how many people report directly to you. There is typically no good reason that you cannot take the first minute out of a work conversation to ask how they are doing. Try to get to know the names of their significant other and any children. Make the effort to get to know their hobbies and passions. Know what their career goals are—both as it relates to working with you today and 10 years down the road.

Everybody wants to know that they matter as a person, that they are not just some cog in the corporate machine. When a supervisor takes such time to get to know them, the results are truly magical. Communication becomes easier, there is more give-and-take with figuring out the best way to accomplish some task, and morale rises. Small actions can yield impressive gains. Human beings spend a third of their day at their job. Productivity soars when they are happy doing it.

I know of one supervisor who kept a meticulous record of everyone's birthday. His assistant always went out to buy the birthday cards, but the supervisor took the time to compose a unique message for everyone's birthday in his department. This simple act may have taken five minutes out of his day, but the heartfelt loyalty he received back from his staff was overwhelming—very much worth it even from a purely efficiency standpoint.

I used the term "management by walking around" in the last chapter, and it has gained a certain amount of traction recently in the corporate world. However, this concept has existed in the military for centuries. How many movies have you seen where the senior leader, whether he is an officer or enlisted, walks amongst the troops and shows he truly cares about their well-being? We do this because it is an effective way to make sure that every one of our troops is on the same page and is part of the team. It also shows that you are part of that team, right there on the ground with them. In the corporate setting, it is just as important, and helps you gauge whether you are moving in the right direction and at the right speed. It will not be along trenches, but it should be "on the ground," among your people. Come down from the higher floors, stray from those parts of the building where everyone wears a suit, visit your people on their terms—they will reward you with loyalty, with production, and with profits.

This is an informal process, but one where you connect with your people. As a result, they will find you approachable and accessible, and that will ultimately pay huge dividends for you. And, just like in the military, this is a great way to pass information to your team and to "gather intelligence" on what is important to them.

I mentioned in an earlier chapter that if my Marines had to clean up an area of a warehouse, I never hesitated to pick up a broom and work right alongside of them. This is something I constantly did, no matter the task. Leading from behind is such an oxymoron. When your people see you in front of them, you will begin propelling them forward. As the saying goes, do not be afraid to roll up your sleeves and get your hands dirty. It is good for your staff, and good for you. It is always helpful to remember what it feels like to do the work you are asking your employees to do. I also saw my Marines take the initiative and implement a number of activities that benefited our unit as a whole. Frankly, I would not have thought of some of them myself, and we all gained from their leadership mentality.

As a leader, you cannot be afraid to ask others to start leading. Leadership is a funny thing. Some people really desire it, and others have it thrust upon them. One of your obligations as a manager is to help others get a taste of leadership and find out who has the strengths and abilities to lead. Much of this is going to depend on the type of work you do, but there are usually opportunities to put others in a leadership role. It may be as the head of a committee in your department or it may be something fun, like planning the company holiday party. You have to remember that one of the roles of a leader is to evaluate the strengths and weaknesses of your people. This applies to their leadership potential, too. I have seen, many times, where someone has the make-up of a good leader, but they do not realize it themselves. By giving these individuals the chance to spread their wings a bit, they can discover their potential—and I can evaluate that potential. This is the result of getting to know who is working for you.

As I mentioned, there are managers that scoff at this concept. For most of these scoffers, they are simply scared of trying their hand at leading others and do not know how to go about it. In such a case, this is where you can see the value of setting the example. The odds are good that supervisors who do not want to embrace this philosophy probably never had one of their managers practice it. Remember, it is the norm to imitate what we are used to, but really good leaders will take the next step of learning something unfamiliar if they believe it may help them. If your corporate culture does not operate with this attitude, then be brave, be the first. There is nothing wrong with being a trendsetter with an idea that works!

You might be reading this and saying to yourself, "Good idea, but that's just not me. I feel uncomfortable getting to know my staff that closely. I don't know how to do it."

Every journey begins with a single, first step. The important thing is to start! It may feel unnatural and a little fake at first, but what you need to do is to make a concentrated effort to lead by example and put your people first whenever you can. The more you do this—and try to make it a habit—the easier it will become until it is second nature. When we combine desire with concrete actions, we can make anything happen.

This is not going to occur overnight, though, especially if this is a foreign concept for you. Some habits take just a few weeks and others take much longer. In one study, the time to change a habit from nonexistent to automatic ranged from 18 days to over 5 months. The average was 66 days, just over 3 months. By the way, you know that a habit is a part of your personality when it starts to feel weird *not* to do it.

When you have the backing of those that work for you, it is so much easier to be successful. Doing well in business means that you coordinate all of the complex factors together in order to market your goods or services and to realize a healthy profit. If you are in a government office or the nonprofit world, success is accomplishing your specific goal as an organization, not achieving a profit, per se. But it is still the result of bringing together many diverse pieces in order to reach that objective. A leader understands his people and knows how to motivate them in order to get all the pieces together and in the right order to achieve the mission.

Being a leader is hard. Anyone who says otherwise has never been a true leader. The differences are in how you want to go about it. It is hard work and takes effort to get to know your people, to constantly remember that you need to set an example in everything you do. It is much harder, though, to have to constantly replace and train new staff if your style of leadership is alienating people instead of getting them to work together.

I once heard a parent with four kids say something that applies to managing in the workplace. He said that the biggest thing he guards against with his kids is not to treat them all the same. In order to get his four kids to grow into their potential, he had to employ four different methods. He could give one something to do and she would run with it. With another, he had to closely work with him before he had the confidence to work on his own. One daughter needed to understand everything before she was comfortable doing something. Another son was capable of almost anything, but needed a kick in the butt to get going. He said these unique facets of their personality stayed with them all through college and adulthood. They are each out on their own and successful today, but if he had not taken the time to understand each child as an individual, he probably would have made some major mistakes in raising them.

Your staff or employees are similarly different. One size does not fit all. If you do not get to know them and if they do not see you leading by example, you will find that your job and ambitions are going to hit one frustration after another. This is a case where putting a little hard work into becoming a better leader will pay off in dividends that you cannot even imagine.

Adopting this as the essence of your leadership will serve you well whether you recently received your first promotion or are on track to become a CEO or start your own company. Sometimes businesses become bogged down in every type of metric imaginable as the strength of the company is measured. These are very helpful tools, but it becomes too easy to forget that there is flesh and blood that makes every metric possible. Military battles talk about casualties, but every leader knows that each one of those casualties is a person and takes that to heart. As a leader in business, that is the same way to look at your employees. Profit, inventory, and anything else you measure are the results of the hard work of people—your people.

KEY TAKEAWAYS

1. Remember what it felt like when a leader put your needs first
    —strive to regularly replicate that.

2. Impactful leaders give others on their teams opportunities to
    lead as well.

3. Do not use a checklist to get to know your people, but show
    your genuine interest in them and the rest will fall into place.

Leading by example is a critical skill, especially in combat. We all learned about the power of mutual respect from Lieutenant Colonel Desgrosseilliers interacting with the local Iraqi leadership.

Our Marines all knew their jobs well, and therefore we could easily switch team members in and out of particular convoys.

CHAPTER 6

TEAMWORK IS CRITICAL FOR SUCCESS, FOR YOU AND FOR OTHERS AROUND YOU

For the strength of the pack is the wolf, and the strength of the wolf is the pack.

Rudyard Kipling — "The Law of the Jungle"

THIS LINE EPITOMIZES THE essence of teamwork. An individual can only do so much alone. A group of individuals can do so much more together, but only if everyone does their job.

I lived this way of life in the Marines. As I have shown, the method of madness in our Marine training was to build trust within the group, whether you were with someone just out of basic training or a battle-tested general. Whatever your role or duty in the Marines, being part of a team was how you accomplished your mission and how you kept people safe. This mindset and training start from your very first days of boot camp or Officer Candidates School and are constantly reinforced throughout your military career.

Look at other aspects of life, too: America is a sports crazy nation. People identify themselves by their favorite teams. While an individual star certainly makes a difference, if the rest of the team is not around him, supporting him and performing at an equally high level, success will be nonexistent. Tom Brady could not win four Super Bowls if he were flat on his back the entire game or his receivers dropped most of his passes. Michael Jordan would not have six NBA championships if he were just one player against five.

Take a look at Hollywood, too. For over a hundred years, stars have been what "makes" the movies. You can have a beautifully written picture, a great director, and a wonderful cinematographer, but the star is usually what people remember. By the same token, if that star did not have the great script, the competent director, and someone to make them look good on film, he might be just the bartender at a local watering hole. Yes, the stars make the money and can carry a picture, but the good ones know that producing a great movie is a total team effort.

Business is no different. A manager may be in a position of responsibility that is critical for the success of the company, but if that person does not utilize the other members of the team, failure is all but guaranteed. We are a society that often puts people on pedestals if they are successful. In some cases, the ones standing on the pedestals may believe their own press clippings and feel they deserve to be there. However, the wise leaders realize that they are up there because of the hard work of everyone involved. They realize that they stand not on a pedestal, at all, but on the collective achievements of their whole team. Delegating the right work to the right people is a critical skill. Instilling the right mentality in those to whom you have delegated closes the loop and reinforces the strengths of the team.

When it comes to the military, sports, business, or anything that requires teamwork for success, I am reminded of a story about the recording of "We Are the World" in 1985. For those too young to remember, this was a charity record made by "everyone who was anyone" in the music business at that time. All of the music stars came to one recording studio for the session. Upon entering the recording studio, the musicians were greeted by a sign pinned to the door that read, "Please check your egos at the door."

This is the attitude you need to hold to be an effective leader. You could very well be managing a group of all-stars in your company. It is great to assemble such talent, but it takes a shrewd leader to bring out the best in everyone. A great leader brings out the best because he knows that the sum of the team's efforts is better than that of any one person. The cliché is usually true that the sum of all the working parts is better than any one component. This means that a leader has to know how to promote teamwork among the group and propel everyone forward into working together. To do this, a leader has to keep his ego in check, as well as having to make sure that everyone else does the same. If you have ever led a group of high achievers, you know this task takes a lot of prior thought and planning. While a leader has certain goals to achieve, he also must understand that he cannot just say, "We are doing it my way or else." Sometimes, sure, that is necessary, but it should not be the default—and certainly not the preferred—management style. Otherwise, you will lose your people, and fast!

The value of teamwork is hard to deny. In leadership training courses, there is an exercise that always proves this fact. The training leader will break the class into groups of four to six people. Each person receives a list of about a dozen items. The scenario everyone is presented with is that they were on a plane that crashed in the wilderness. As individuals, they are to prioritize the items on the list of what is most important to their survival. When they have finished, they then have to decide, as a team, the priority of the items. Whenever this exercise is carried out, 98% of the time the group decision is closer to the correct answer than the answer of any one individual.

In the Marines, this teamwork concept starts from the smallest patrol up to the entire body of the Corps. We drill on doing our job well, and we expect the Marine next to us to be equally proficient in his responsibility. The enlisted Marines know that virtually every officer has gone through the demanding Officer Candidates School, and the officers know how challenging the enlisted boot camp is—this very fact helps establish the trust necessary for teamwork. Professional proficiency also breeds trust because each and every Marine knows that if they do not do their job to the best of their ability, they will be letting their comrades down. Nowhere is this stressed more than in combat, where unsatisfactory performance can result in the most final of results. Working hard for those around you promotes a very dynamic relationship where the sum is stronger than all of the parts. Fostering teamwork is what a leader strives to do.

Teamwork is the only reason I am alive today to write this book. I still am in awe of the teamwork it took to save my life. Here is how Jay Price (a reporter who was with our group that day in Iraq) later described it in an article he wrote:

Bullet in the face

Two minutes later, when the patrol stopped so Lt. Col. Todd Desgrosseilliers could check in with a team of Marines with tanks, a Marine stepped from his Humvee and walked toward the tanks. The snap of a shot rang out from about 150 yards away in the direction of a mosque, houses and shops.

The bullet hit just under the left side of the Marine's jaw and passed through his mouth, knocking out teeth and exiting through his right cheek. He fell to the pavement and a pool of blood began spreading around his head.

The shooting continued.

Cpl. Mario Huerta, 22, of Dallas, was outside his Humvee when he heard the first shot and looked back. A bullet whirred just above him, then another smacked into the goggles on his Kevlar helmet, rocking his head and denting the goggles but not hurting him.

Desgrosseilliers, who earned a Silver Star two years ago in Fallujah, turned when he heard the initial shot. He saw that the burly Marine was down and sprinted nearly 100 yards, ignoring the bullets zipping past his head.

Desgrosseilliers was the first to get to the wounded Marine, whose name can't be divulged under mili-

tary press rules, and he rolled him onto his back. He was joined by Navy corpsman George Grant, 25, of Brooklyn, as shots zipped past their heads.

Desgrosseilliers ordered the Humvees into a circle to block the shots. Then he and Grant ran a breathing tube up the wounded man's nose so he would not drown in his own blood.

The closest field hospital was about four miles back, down a road where improvised bombs are common. Desgrosseilliers' Humvee took the lead, its siren blaring to clear the road.

Within eight minutes, the jump team slid to a stop in front of the surgical unit at an air base near Camp Habbaniyah. Desgrosseilliers joined several jump-team Marines and orderlies in carrying the wounded man inside on a stretcher.

After a few minutes, Grant came out, blood all over his jumpsuit, and sat on the ground, wordless.

A doctor told Grant the Marine likely would live, that he had been stabilized, and would be flown to a larger hospital.

Most people wounded in war do not have the luxury of reading the play-by-play events happening to, and around them, after the injury. What should strike you, as it does me, is that rank became irrelevant to the people who leaped to my aid. I had a senior Marine officer and a mid-level Navy corpsman working on me at the same time. And this was not just a "regular" lieutenant colonel, but the commander of the entire battalion. Not only was he leading from the front as he always did, but still exposed himself to enemy fire and death, the same as Corpsman Grant. Remember, the sniper was still shooting at the rest of the squad, and even hit the Marine behind me. All of these military men responded from their training, knowing that everyone else was doing the same. Leaping to my aid as Corpsman Grant and Lieutenant

Colonel Desgrosseilliers did was indicative of the teamwork mentality the military impresses on its members.

While I was recovering from my wounds, I reached out to Corpsman George Grant to send me his impressions of all that occurred that day. This is what he sent to me:

We started the mission and had made two stops prior to the last one. Shortly after dismounting the vehicle, you walked a few yards forward of your vehicle. I turned my head as I heard a shot fired. I can almost swear I saw you drop as I was taking cover. Colonel Desgrosseilliers was between our position and yours and started running towards you. There was at least one more shot that caused him to seek cover behind a vehicle. Myself, Cpl Huerta, the reporter, and I believe a Marine from the OP took cover behind a vehicle that was in front of us. Cpl Huerta pushed the reporter into a vehicle for his safety. The vehicle pulled off and Cpl Huerta let out a shout. He had been hit in the head with a round or a projectile, breaking his goggles but not injuring him.

At that point, I ran towards your position. I believe Colonel Desgrosseilliers was kneeling to your side, as you were facedown. We turned you over and I saw that your eyes were open but you were unresponsive. There was a lot of damage to your face and there was blood and bubbles coming from what was left of your airway. To be honest, I thought you were dead. I then turned you onto your side, reached into my med pack and placed a nasal trumpet into your airway. I wasn't sure whether you had a pulse or not, and you definitely weren't breathing, so I radioed to Corporal Buhler to bring the vehicle to me and to tear down the spine board that was suspended in the back of the vehicle. I asked Lieutenant Mueller to get the folded stretcher from one of the Marines and to bring it to me. We took away your gear and I decided that the trumpet was probably not going to be very effective with your facial injuries, and that I needed to secure an airway for CPR. I again went into my pack, took out a Combi-tube, and inserted it as the Marines prepared the stretcher. We then rolled you onto the stretcher and lifted you into my vehicle (one of the most difficult things in the world).

I jumped in and took out the ambu-bag and attached it to the tube as we pulled off. I tried to check for placement, but couldn't hear clearly over the background noise and the high speed driving, so I pumped the bag a couple more times until I thought I heard air. I turned you back onto your side and tried to reassess you. While doing that, you woke up, and became combative. You were gagging on the tube and reaching for it, and I was trying to calm you down. The vehicle was cutting through one of the serpentines and you were being thrown around the vehicle so we had to slow the MEDEVAC so that Corporal Buhler could drive safely while helping to hold you. You pulled the tube out but we were able to calm you down. I told you what had happened and that I needed to take care of your wounds.

You seemed to understand what I was saying and who I was, and complied. You kept gesturing at your throat and chest as if you were having difficulty breathing so I told you that I was going to put another airway in and I wanted you to not pull it out. After I placed it, I asked if your breathing had become better and you nodded. Then I applied dressings to your wounds while Buhler and I kept talking to you and keeping you attentive. We pulled onto the base and I explained to you that we were about to be at the Shock Trauma Platoon (STP), and that you needed to get out and sit on the backboard or lay on your side. You again nodded as if you understood, and did exactly that when the doctors and nurses came to get you. They carted you off as I stood there and watched, kind of in shock at the ordeal.

Everything kind of became a blur, I think. I am not sure if Major Leonard was at the STP, or back at the base when we left TQ, but he was the first person I remember walking up to me and cleaning your blood off of my face. I was covered in it but had not realized that. He told me that you were still alive and would probably survive.

I would not trade in the team of professionals who helped me at the worst time of my life for all of the championship teams in the world. The dedication of everyone from that day is awe-inspiring. While this was far from a typical day for me, how everyone around me acted in the aftermath of me being shot was not out of the ordinary. Every action taken in response to my injuries would have been the same for anyone else. Actually, I was the first case of such traumatic damage that the doctors had seen. But their training took over and they worked together to stop incredible bleeding and to "package" me (literally, they packed my wounds with gauze and then packed me and the massive amount of medical monitoring and IV equipment keeping me alive from second to second into a three-layered body bag as tightly as they could so I could survive the trip to Balad) for the trip to a real hospital. My case was then used to develop the protocol that forward surgical unit used in treating the too many other cases of such traumatic injury the doctors would see over the course of their tours. In that crisis, though, it was the teamwork of my unit and then of the unit of doctors and surgeons that saved my life. And, the point is, the training and the mentality of all those that saved me that day could have manifested itself in any situation they were faced with—I am lucky they came together for me that day.

You may very well be in a profession where life and death situations are a possibility, like the police force, first responders, the medical field, etc. However, most jobs are not fraught with those crisis issues. Wherever you work, though, recognize the importance of a leader promoting the type of teamwork that I experienced when those around me saved my life. If you can make that happen, you will go far in your profession.

Face it: No matter the company or organization you work for, a crisis can spring up any day. Quite often, it probably feels like there is one every day! On the grand scale of life, it may not seem important, but it is certainly significant for you and something that you have to resolve. Would you rather be in a position where every crisis is one that you have to deal with alone, or would you rather have a good team of people around you to apply their collective talents to the problem?

I only recently was able to speak to the team of doctors that treated and packaged me that day. I asked them specifically about the training they received that allowed them to work so effectively together. Dr. Christopher's response, I think, is particularly instructive. He told me that when he was just learning his craft, he was in an ICU. He told me that, sometimes, it was one or two patients with really traumatic injuries and four doctors—in those instances, he drew valuable lessons from watching the very experienced doctors handle a crisis. At other times, though, there would be four or five incredibly traumatic injuries, each requiring attention NOW—in those instances, he learned valuable lessons from having to act. He was forced to handle a real crisis—that was his best training for what he saw when I was carried into his surgical unit in the desert on that October day.

Another of the doctors told me something equally insightful that I think is important to pass along. Dr. Bilski told me that their training actually told them that they would have to place a surgical airway (that they would have to cut into my throat to allow for a breathing tube to be inserted). In that moment, though, they saw that my soft tissue could simply be moved out of the way to allow for a tube to pass into my lungs. Note, here, that training and training and training makes you ready for what you have trained for; but that training does not necessarily dictate every action. Rather the circumstances in which you find yourself must dictate your exact response. Part of the value of training is to identify what is or is not out of place in a situation and to react accordingly. That day, all my doctors came together and, with all their collective training, knew just what to do and reacted, saving my life so that Corpsman Grant could be told that the man whose blood covered his face, arms, and uniform, was going to live.

Teamwork is often the difference between a great company or department and one with many deficiencies. But teamwork does not just develop overnight. Developing effective teams is the single most important role of a leader. A leader has to develop that teamwork among the people reporting to her. "Working together" is not just an empty concept. It is a concrete methodology for getting the job done. A proactive leader strives every day toward getting the team to work together and for each member of the group to learn that each can depend upon and trust one another. It may take significant effort and time to achieve this, but once you do, you as the leader will find success—and so will each member of the team.

I have actually heard managers say, "I am not evaluated on promoting teamwork." They say they are rated on productivity, or profit margin, or whatever metric the company is using, but not teamwork as such. This is shortsighted. Sustained success occurs only when the person in charge spends the time necessary to figure out how to reach the organization's goals. When a group supports and believes in its members, the team members are going to meet their goals and metrics almost as a byproduct of their working well together. As long as the leadership promotes teamwork in conjunction with a sound plan in the first place, then the odds of meeting all goals increase dramatically.

I want to emphasize again that numbers and metrics do not determine leadership. Rather, leadership developing teamwork, trust, and the right attitude is how you get people to work toward those numbers and metrics. It is all about *people*, your people. As a leader, you may need to develop techniques and a personality to work with people better than you have in the past. Remember, the more you practice anything, the easier that thing gets. Through thought and effort, you will be able to pull a group together so they act as one. At that point, you are well on your way to being an impactful and effective leader.

KEY TAKEAWAYS

1. A chain is only as strong as its weakest link. Ensure that you are engaging everyone on your team and that you are enabling each of them to operate at their highest level.

2. As a leader, you will encounter more than one crisis. Make sure that you and the rest of your team have prepared for these situations.

3. Everyone on a team has a different role, and together they can achieve so much more than any individual accomplishment.

Dahlia and I incorporate every aspect of teamwork into our relationship, both consciously and subconsciously, which is what it has taken for a successful recovery after that sniper's bullet. By the time I received my Purple Heart medal, Dahlia had been such a key part of my recovery that I viewed it as our injury and our award. Therefore, I thought it entirely appropriate to have her next to me when I received the award.

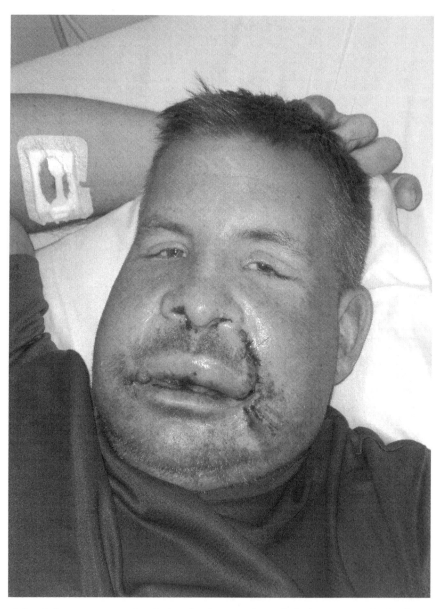

I had the wrong attitude in the hospital and did not want help from anybody. This picture was from a year after I was shot, when the doctors removed the fibula bone from my left leg and used it to reconstruct my upper jaw.

CHAPTER 7

IT IS OKAY TO ASK FOR HELP AND
TO LEAN ON OTHERS FOR SUPPORT

Pride Goeth Before the Fall.

— Proverbs 16:18

THE ACTUAL VERSE IS, according to the King James Bible, "Pride goeth before destruction, and an haughty spirit before a fall." In other words, if you believe that any success you have is solely due to your own efforts, then sooner or later you are going to be sitting on your butt, watching everyone else pass you by. I touched on this concept in the last chapter when I talked about teamwork. If a leader believes that he can do everything without their team, then any success is going to be short-lived.

There is another way that pride can cut you off at the knees. That can happen when people feel that they are so self-reliant, it must be a sign of weakness to ask anybody for help. Usually, whether in life or business, a person learns this lesson the hard way when 20/20 hindsight kicks into gear. How often have you heard, or said it yourself, "If I had only asked for some advice or help."

"Leading" is not knowing all of the answers. And it is definitely not making up the answers. I have never heard of anyone criticized for saying, "I don't know the answer to that right now. But I will find out, and get back to you." Instead of criticism, there is usually a great deal of respect for such honesty.

Remember, successful leadership depends on having the best information possible in order to make a decision. Obtaining that data often means that you need to seek out the members of your group, go to a superior, or use an outside source. Anyone in the military or on successful teams can tell you that it is imperative to rely on others for information, support, and guidance.

I had this lesson served up to me on a platter in the aftermath of my injury. When I started the recovery process, I did not want help from anybody. I woke up in the hospital and wanted nothing more than to be back with my Marines in Iraq. I felt that being so far from my team, being stuck in the United States, was Mission Failure. I was completely embarrassed about what had happened. In fact, I told my family not to invite my friends to the hospital—I just wanted to deal with my issues by myself. My journey to learning this lesson was a long one, an odyssey with many hard days made harder by my stubborn, and stupid, resolve to try to recover by myself. My experience learning this lesson gives me a great platform to tell you now: Do not be afraid to reach out to others for support.

I am only here today because of all of those wonderful people in Iraq who saved my life. As you can guess, I did not have any say about what should happen immediately after I was shot. I am grateful to all of the personnel who helped, racing to my aid. Then there were the doctors, nurses, and therapists that helped me after the day of the injury—people to whom I owe so much for how successful my recovery has been. Dr. Eduardo Rodriguez in particular, my incredibly gifted plastic surgeon from Johns Hopkins University, not only made me feel much more confident in the long road to recovery I was facing, but did the same for a number of other severely wounded warriors as well. In the beginning of this rehabilitation process, however, I certainly did not want to ask for help. I do not know if it was pride, stubbornness, or just plain being scared of the uphill battle I was facing, but asking for help was something I had to learn slowly.

I have had over 25 surgeries and I still have a few more to go. My first surgery was 19 hours long. Over the years, the medical teams have removed the fibula bones from both my legs to reconstruct my upper and lower jaws. They reconstructed my injured head and performed surgery on my cornea to try to remove the scar tissue from my retina. They completely rebuilt my mouth, including using part of my hip and bone marrow to strengthen the supports around my new dentures. Each of these surgeries had varying degrees of success. Anyone who has had any kind of injury or procedure in a hospital knows that the hardest part is all of the rehabilitation work that comes after surgery.

As you can guess, I had a long road to rehab ahead of me. Before the injury, I had been working out with hundreds of pounds in the gym in Iraq—remember, I was the "burly Marine." After being shot, though, I had to do bicep curls in my hospital room with just five-pound weights. I was in a wheelchair for quite a while, and then on crutches for even longer. Talking intelligibly with almost no teeth, while also missing the end of my tongue was practically impossible. I remember drawing a picture so my then-girlfriend, now-wife Dahlia could scratch an itch on my back. And because I had no lower teeth, I constantly drooled (and still do to some extent to this day), which was the most embarrassing aspect of my recovery. To get through all of this, I had to depend on the many medical personnel I met during that time. I had to trust their instructions and their words of encouragement. Formerly, my tendency would probably have been for people to just leave me alone to recover on my own. I realized, though, that doing that would have been a disaster. I recognized the fact that I had to lean on the people who knew their stuff. The more I leaned on them, the easier it was for me to ask questions. I got really good at being a sponge—I gathered every speck of information that could potentially hasten my recovery.

It was not easy. In fact, when I speak to various audiences about my successful transition and celebration of life, they often ask me about if I had and how I dealt with my "dark days" during that time. I certainly had my share, both in the hospital and later as an outpatient.

When I first arrived at the National Naval Medical Center in Bethesda, Maryland, my head was so incredibly swollen that, not only was it hard to recognize me, but I also could not talk. In fact, it took me several weeks to get out my first word. The doctors actually considered whether Corpsman Grant had accidentally cut my vocal cord when he performed that battlefield tracheostomy (which would have been perfectly understandable under those harrowing circumstances). I was in the ICU, had not slept in a week, had a temperature of almost 104 degrees, was experiencing what is called ICU syndrome, and was put on Ambien to help me sleep. Very unfortunately, as it turned out, we did not know at the time that I was incredibly allergic to Ambien.

Before I describe what happened next, I need to explain to you a little bit about my tracheostomy. A tracheostomy is an artificial opening in the neck into the windpipe (trachea). It allows air to go in and out of the lungs. It also allows any mucus to be removed. A small tube (the tracheostomy tube) is inserted through this opening. Breathing occurs through this tube. A tracheostomy collar (commonly called a trach—pronounced "trake"—collar) is a soft plastic mask that fits over and around the tracheostomy tube, allowing humidified air and oxygen to be delivered.

It was always very disturbing for me when the doctors had to adjust my trach collar. Not only was it painful, but it felt like they were pushing something deep inside my chest. Also, the nurses would periodically remove the trach collar and then stick a thin rod down that hole to cause me to cough violently, which was the primary way to remove the mucus that developed there. At the time, I was quite proud of the blood splatter on the wall 10 feet away from my bed caused by some of that coughing!

Unfortunately, I had two separate medical teams checking on my trach collar, and they disagreed about the particular type of collar I should use. So, every time one of them came in, they would change out the old trach collar and put a different one in. This was incredibly painful for me, completely unnecessary, and would be a major factor in the horrible hallucinations I suffered later.

The Ambien did help me fall asleep, but the combination of my allergic reaction to it, my ICU syndrome, and my dangerously high temperature caused me to have incredibly detailed and horrifying hallucinations. In each of them, it was almost impossible for me to breathe, no doubt from the constant pain in my throat. In one scenario, I had been hijacked by a medical team and was taken to a slum in Mexico where they performed high-risk experimental surgeries on me. For some reason, my best friend was there with me. Not only did we both have problems breathing, but the medical team left us with just one oxygen tank to make our way back to the United States. One tank was only enough for one of us to make it, and I had to decide how to apportion the oxygen. In another scenario of these recurring nightmares, some members of the hospital staff (who, apparently, I did not like in my subconscious) were part of an elaborate conspiracy to defraud the American public and the patients in the hospital. Meanwhile, other members of the staff (who I apparently *did* like in my subconscious) led a daring and high-risk raid to bring me to safety before I died from suffocation.

Right now, in the light of day these stories just sound silly, but at the time they could not have been more real or scarier. In fact, I can still remember sitting in my chair and truly believing that a face in the ceiling was talking to me and that the family in a picture on the wall jumped into my room when nobody was looking. I also wrote a note to my friends (I could not talk at the time) to please move my chair because too much rain was coming in through the window and I was getting wet. In reality, there was no window in my room. Ultimately, my nightmares were so disturbing that they caused my heart to beat more than 100 times per minute (I normally have a resting heart rate of about 50 beats per minute). The doctors told Dahlia and my family that if they could not fix the situation, then I would likely have a heart attack and die. Fortunately, they identified what was happening and changed my medication. My condition was soon much more manageable.

Surprisingly, I was only in the hospital for five weeks before they released me to my house as an outpatient. At that time, wounded Marines desperately needed the bed space, and the nurses taught Dahlia how to thoroughly clean out the inside of my mouth. This included a suction device, lollipop sponges, gauze, and endless patience. Because we lived within easy driving distance of the hospital, I would return regularly for surgeries and periodic examinations. Along the way, though, I had to get used to asking for help in every aspect of my life.

Because the doctors had removed the fibula from my right leg during that original surgery, and despite my rehab regimen, I struggled with walking "normally" for a long time. I went home in a wheelchair, just as I did a year later after another major surgery removing the fibula from my left leg to reconstruct my upper jaw. Both times, I "graduated" to crutches and had to use those for quite some time, too. Unfortunately, in our townhouse at the time, as soon as you walked in, you had to walk up two flights of stairs to get to the living area, and then another flight to the bedrooms. That was hard work with crutches, but not as hard as getting used to asking for help with washing myself, getting dressed and undressed, going anyplace at all, making and taking phone calls (it was practically impossible for anyone to understand me over the phone—Dahlia always had to help), getting anything from across the room, and the list only goes on.

In fact, just eating was a wholly new and challenging experience. I was on a feeding tube for months, and they sent us home with hundreds of cans of Ensure protein drink. I "ate" by having Dahlia pour the drink into a funnel attached to my feeding tube, and the liquid went straight to my stomach. Sometimes before pouring the Ensure, Dahlia would jokingly ask whether I wanted chocolate, strawberry, or vanilla, as if I could taste any of it. It was actually rather funny at the time, and we learned to laugh at these situations pretty regularly. To this day, I have a greatly diminished sense of taste and smell, and therefore Dahlia not only makes food that is extra flavorful so that I can enjoy it, but soft enough so that it does not hurt my very sensitive upper palette. This is what now makes our meals together extra special. Her particular care and attention mean so much to me.

I became so much better at learning to ask for help in these intervening years that, at this point, I have reached out to at least a dozen different veterans' organizations for assistance. They have all been wonderful. Even though we still have a long way to go, America does a good job of helping our veterans. It has made a big difference in my life and I now try to do all I can for these groups.

The physical process of rebuilding was only one aspect of my rehabilitation. In addition to what the sniper's bullet did to my body, I identified that I had PTS. Just like dealing with my physical wounds, it was difficult at first for me to wrap my head around this issue and ask for the help that I needed. But I realized that I could handle it in one of two ways. I could go talk to an objective professional who had worked with other warriors before, somebody who had researched these issues and could help explain why my mind and body were behaving and reacting as they were. The alternative was to keep my problems bottled up inside and just see what happened. Not only has asking for help on this very personal issue helped me individually, but now I have been invited by the Veterans Affairs, the Marine Corps, the Wounded Warrior Project, and other groups to talk publicly about PTS in an effort to help others who are alone in their battles, taking on the demons in their heads one-on-one. I really enjoy knowing that I am helping other Veterans. It is a huge positive boost for me that only happened because I took that first step and asked for help.

The approach I took in recovering from a wound on the battlefield is a metaphor for how leadership needs to operate in business. Life does not go smoothly. You can run into a problem, some difficulty, or opposition to what you are trying to accomplish any or every day. The truth is that you are not going to know the solution to every problem. So you will have to ask for help. For some people, that can be very difficult. As I pointed out, above, this is something that you can learn to do. As with most behaviors, the more you do it, the easier it becomes.

If you have trouble leaning on others or asking for help, try to look at the problem logically. If you are facing a problem that you do not know how to conquer, what are your options? You can try to march forward through the problem, conquering the thing through sheer force of will. But the odds are good that your lack of knowledge concerning the issue means that tactic will fail. Sure, you may temporarily hide the fact that you needed help in the first place, but this course of action will usually land you in hot water. On the other hand, you can seek out help from those who have different information or expertise, solve the problem, and get on with your job. Looking at it that way, are stubborn pride or fear of embarrassment worth it? I think not. Looking back, I wish I had not been so embarrassed about what happened to me. I would hate for anyone else to make that same mistake.

Within our military community—but across American society, generally, too—we do not like to talk about behavioral health issues. Although nearly 24 million Americans are suffering from some sort of behavioral health issue right now, it is not a topic most feel comfortable discussing. It is perfectly natural for someone who breaks her arm to go see a doctor, but we do not, unfortunately but certainly still, have the same attitude for those suffering from some mental health issue. Therefore, I often tell my friends in the military that asking for help shows maturity and confidence. I tell them that it is a sign of strength, not weakness. And I mean it.

Being a true leader often means having to do things you do not want to do, taking actions you are not comfortable performing. You have to keep at the forefront of your mind that the goal of any leader is to reach the objectives of the organization. There are always multitudes of objectives for every level of management in a company. Some goals can be more difficult to achieve than others. And people know that. So never be afraid to reach out for help when you need it. Doing so indicates that you are a mature leader. If you are worried that your supervisor may look at your asking for advice or assistance as a negative thing, you have to realize that he became your leader because that is what he did on his way up the ranks. Consequently, keep this lesson in mind when a member of your team reaches out to you.

After all, you should understand that your role as a leader means being there when your staff comes to you. That is your job. It is one of the responsibilities you may have looked forward to when getting into a leadership role. It makes sense that your leader(s) would feel that way in their relationship with you. They want to be there to help you if you need it. By helping you through an issue, the larger goals—their goals—are advanced. This is how a good organization thrives. Everyone pulls for everyone else, toward a common goal. There is no room for jealousy, ego, pride, or floundering around with a problem when there are good people to go to for help.

It is also important to keep in mind that not all of your answers may come from above you. One of the advantages of getting to know your team is that you learn their strengths and weaknesses. As a leader, the reason you want to have everyone perform as a unit is so that their strengths and weaknesses can complement one another. One person's weakness is another person's strength. You as a leader should know everyone's strong points. You can channel those strengths into meeting the team's objectives. The sad truth is that many poor leaders are just that simply because they do not realize the resources they have in their own people.

I would bet that the main reason my small team in Iraq was so successful in the civil affairs projects we took on was because of how effective my Marines were, both individually and together. I was lucky enough to have a fair number of soldiers that had already deployed to Iraq, so they provided a good base of knowledge. I could leave for a two-day mission with the battalion commander and have complete confidence that my non-commissioned officers would ensure that all necessary tasks and goals were accomplished. We often worked shoulder to shoulder on the most mundane tasks like cleaning out old storage facilities, but those actions brought us closer together. I grew to rely heavily on Sergeant Howard—whom I had met just months before—and because I could lean on him, I could free my time for other aspects of our mission.

A good leader does not put himself on a pedestal; he puts the men and women who report to him up on that stand. You know, there is a big difference between being a boss and being a leader. First, did you realize that boss spelled backward is a double s.o.b.? Kidding aside, a person with a "boss" mentality tends to push his people without regard to their own success. A leader, on the other hand, is there to help them do well and to help teach everyone on the team how to use their potential.

Take a moment to think about this if you still feel funny about asking for help: Do you like helping other people? When friends of yours have turned to you with a serious issue in the past, what have you done? You probably stopped whatever you were doing and focused on your friend, just like George Grant did for me when I needed it most. Well, that is the kind of reception you should receive when you seek help from a trusted supervisor, a member of your staff, a good friend, or a coworker. And that is the reception you must grant to each of those people, as well, both up and down the hierarchy. There is no reason for any of us to walk around fighting battles by ourselves when help is only a conversation away.

At the same time, never forget that you are stronger than you think you are. In the Marine Corps, they train us very hard to be tough, efficient, and extremely resilient. Physical and mental fitness is a part of everything we do. Although I felt like I was in good shape when I started Officer Candidates School and had been playing competitive rugby for 10 years, I lost 20 pounds in 10 weeks, and left OCS a different person. If someone had described to me the workout regimen we would be doing there, I would have said that there was no way I could keep up. And before I deployed to Iraq, if someone could have truly described what it is like to carry 65 pounds of protective armor, two weapons, and hundreds of rounds of ammunition, all in more than 100-degree weather, and then to routinely conduct long foot patrols for four or five hours at a given stretch, I probably would have said that I couldn't do that, either. But I could. And I did.

While all that training certainly helped me to deal with my hardships after the injury, I still had to reach down to physical and emotional resources I did not know I possessed. I had strength to do a lot on my own. But I still needed help. In every instance throughout my journey, people responded when I reached out. Because of their help, I was able to achieve my goals.

You will run into the same circumstances in business. Leadership brings you into situations that are definitely outside your comfort zone. You are competent, sure, but you are not on an island. A great leader learns how to use the resources at his disposal, and this often means making the most of the people we work with every day. There are going to be tough times as a leader, but we are all stronger than we think and we can each do great things. Together, though, we can accomplish amazing things.

KEY TAKEAWAYS

1. Not asking for help is counterproductive, shortsighted and can adversely affect others.

2. Even the most successful person needs help at different points throughout her life.

3. A mature leader truly does have an open door policy.

Because of my personal experience with Post Traumatic Stress, I participated in a bipartisan effort to change the national conversation about mental health issues in America.

This is what I looked like before I was shot. Dahlia and I were on our first date in Buenos Aires, Argentina, and I ordered a huge meal for myself of their famous BBQ, not realizing she was a vegetarian!

CHAPTER 8

CHANGE IS OPPORTUNITY

NOTHING IN LIFE REMAINS constant. We are continually chang-ing, adapting, evolving. This is true in our personal as well as in our professional lives. Nine years ago, my life changed dramatically. By all objective measures, I should not have survived to be here today. I imagine everyone reading this book has experienced some kind of significant change during their lives, and so might be able to relate to some of the following true examples of sudden, unexpected change:

Imagine that you are in the world of dating and you meet a terrific person. You have two or three great times together. This may be the "significant other" or your "other half" that you have been hoping to find. All of a sudden, he receives a promotion that whisks them to the other side of the country. And, boom, you are single again.

Now imagine that a business presentation is due and you prepare it with attention given to every detail. You show a great PowerPoint presentation and there is just no reason your prospective client should not buy into it. But you used a picture of the New York Mets to dress up one of your slides emphasizing the teamwork of your company, and the client is a diehard Yankee fan. He politely shows you the door.

Or maybe you have worked for the same company for 20 years and worked your way up to vice president. You have 10 more years ahead of you before you are able to retire at a fairly young age. Then, one day, you get off a plane while traveling to a business meeting and take a call from your boss, the owner of your company. He just sold the business! Great news for him, but they only want your company's contracts and not any of the people. Uh-oh!!

The Greek philosopher Heraclitus said, "Change is the only constant in life." We see this all around us, in every aspect of our existence. It affects our families, business, government, hobbies, travel—everything. I believe a person's ability to embrace and positively react to change is one of the biggest determinations of how life will proceed for that individual.

How a leader deals with change is a factor in how her people will remember her. Successful leadership is all about anticipating, reacting to, and taking advantage of changes as they pop up on our radar. Do not get me wrong here. I am not saying that a successful leader can see every change before it happens. Nobody can do that. But a great leader will not look at change as a roadblock or as a negative. Instead, it is an opportunity to make something even better than originally anticipated. As the cliché goes, if life gives you lemons, make lemonade.

As you may have guessed, I took on a truckload of lemons the day I was shot. To illustrate the randomness of change, I am going to take the spotlight off me for a bit and look at two other individuals who were there with me that day. We need only look to the 20 seconds before and 20 seconds after the sniper targeted me to illustrate just how random events can affect individuals.

Remember the reporter who was out there with us that day? His name is Jay Price and I had noticed that he was kind of standing around, not continually moving to avoid being an easy target for a sniper. When we got out of the vehicle and started walking away from the Humvee, I told Jay that he needed to move faster or that he might get shot. Based on that, he took a big step forward. A split second later, a round came in right where his head had been, hitting the wall behind us. The next shot hit me right behind my ear and exited out my mouth. The reporter was unharmed. Then, as Price reported, *Cpl. Mario Huerta, 22, of Dallas, was outside his Humvee when he heard the first shot and looked back. A bullet whirred just above him, then another smacked into the goggles on his Kevlar helmet, rocking his head and denting the goggle, but not hurting him.* Huerta was unharmed, as well.

In the incredibly short period of time before and after I was hit, the sniper could have made three kill shots. Instead, the sniper missed Jay entirely and Corporal Huerta should send a "thank you" note to the manufacturers of his helmet and goggles. But a bullet did hit me and I have had to face years of profound changes. Such are the building blocks of life.

I wish I had that bullet. I would like to keep it on my shelf, reminding me that I will never face anything as terrible as that one little bullet. It is funny that something so small can be so destructively powerful. For me, though, that is empowering. I could not control that bullet, but I can control what I do now because of it. I do wish I had that bullet to hold up, look at, weigh in my hand, and to toss up and down.

How I confronted this change in my life is the lesson I want others to think about and apply to their own circumstances. A major part of my health and successful recovery was my conscious decision to accept what happened to me. With acceptance, we also recognize our strengths and our vulnerabilities. We can then set realistic life goals based on our "new normal." We all probably want to go back in time and do something differently in life. For me, it would have been as simple as stepping a foot to the right. However, except in science fiction, there are no time machines. So either we are going to waste way too much of our precious time wishing we could go back, or we can choose to focus on today and the future and on moving past whatever obstacle has gotten in our way.

Many times, when we face change, it forces us to come up with both short-term and long-term solutions to the situation. My short-term concerns were for my health and rehabilitation. I have now had more than 25 reconstructive surgeries. My first surgery back in the States was 19 hours long. The doctors told my family that if they had waited 12 more hours to perform that surgery, my whole face would have collapsed from the extensive damage. Because the doctors had to remove bones from my legs to reconstruct my entire mouth, the simple act of walking was a huge challenge for quite some time, as was talking, any sort of exercise, or feeling comfortable in crowds.

I will give you an example of one of the basic human activities where I have had to make what has been perhaps my most major adjustment, eating. The bullet destroyed most of my teeth and the end of my tongue. Due to nerve damage in my face, I cannot now feel if I have food around my mouth, which—trust me—can be quite embarrassing. And despite my best efforts, due to my reshaped mouth, I still drool at various times throughout the day, but cannot feel it. Most of my bottom teeth are now dentures, as are my upper teeth, except for four molars. In fact, it took six years of reconstruction before my orthodontic surgeon, Dr. Ghassan Sinada, was able to fit me for upper dentures, finally allowing me to actually bite into a piece of food. He was one of my excellent doctors from Johns Hopkins University, and typically operated on patients with debilitating injuries from cancer. Ultimately, those upper dentures turned out to be uncomfortable, so I have just adapted to eating and talking without any upper teeth (except for those molars).

I gave some details in a past chapter about the medical difficulties I went through. If it had not been for the love, support, and teamwork of family, friends, and a long list of medical professionals, I never could have navigated that sea of change, trying to get body and soul back together again. It is an ongoing process that I continue to deal with every day.

I do not want you to think that my entire life revolved around my medical situation. I had other important life issues to think about, like making a living. I enjoyed my attorney positions with the Department of Justice, on Capitol Hill, and with the FBI, but I wanted more. Starting my own business as a leadership advisor and an inspirational speaker was the best thing that could have happened to me. However, I cannot say this was part of my career plan before my tour in Iraq. But when you are given lemons . . . you get the picture.

Besides my business, I recently finished an advanced law degree at Georgetown University and graduated with honors. Prior to my injury, I was never a particularly great student. Afterward, however, I realized how important every day is and how critical it is to never squander an opportunity. I also now do a great deal of volunteer work with a number of different groups. This drastic change in my life has resulted in me helping all kinds of people I probably never would have before (e.g., adult literacy tutoring, boards of directors, helping individual wounded warriors, peer mentoring, etc.). I also recently co-founded the Veteran Success Resource Group—a nonprofit organization to help many more of our service members and their families on a much larger scale.

I am sure you can understand how being a Marine and my own personal circumstances made me an easy advocate for many veterans' and wounded warriors' groups. When I was in Iraq, our constant foot patrols, combined with the intense heat and carrying 65 pounds of weapons and gear, made for long days. Every day presented a very real danger of stepping on or driving over an IED, engaging in deadly firefights with a determined enemy, or not making it into a bunker before incoming rockets and mortars exploded.

I still remember a memorial service in our unit, not long after I arrived in Iraq. I stood in the back of the packed, stuffy room and looked down the aisle at the six sets of boots, rifles, helmets, and dog tags. I had seen these young men hug each other before heading out on patrol—real hugs, as if they might not see each other again. They had been in Iraq for a while and knew how dangerous every mission was.

I asked the battalion commander how he dealt with memorial services for Marines who looked like they could still be in high school. He sighed, looked down, and said that it never gets any easier. Although it never gets any easier for me to think about it, I do not want to forget those young men.

One of the ways I chose to channel the many changes in my life into something good is to support a wide variety of people who are facing tough challenges in their lives. Most people with injuries like mine do not live to talk about it. I know that this is my second lease on life and, because I know that, am now much more empathetic toward others. Whether it is other wounded warriors, the children at my wife's school who face daunting personal circumstances, or those struggling to find fulfilling work, I do everything I can to find ways to help. I have so much I am trying to accomplish because I know that life is sweet, precious, and something we should treasure, not just get through.

This is certainly a battlefield lesson every leader should take to heart. Change is inevitable. How you react to it is going to make or break you, and also the people in your circle. The reaction you have to change is directly related to how you think of the word.

For too many people, the word "change" has a negative connotation. At first, change certainly can be challenging to embrace. This is where you need to step up to the plate. A leader needs to analyze what happened and, more importantly, how to get things going again. A poor leader says, "Woe is me. Why can't things be the way they always were?" A good leader says, "We are moving in a new direction now. This is exciting."

The bottom line is that life changes for better or for worse. Which depends only on how you choose to look at it. I choose for the glass to be half-full, not half-empty, every morning. I choose to embrace change. I want to live in the future, not the past. I am not defined by what happened to me, but how I have dealt with the change that has come along with it. I have learned that through inner strength, humility, and a victorious spirit, we can each overcome the toughest obstacles.

If a leader understands that gradual or sudden change is a part of life, then she will adopt a positive attitude toward dealing with change. The results will generally be constructive and her business or organization will flourish all the more. Conversely, someone who ignores the winds of change or hangs on for things to return to "the good old days" is the equivalent of an ostrich with its head in the sand.

If you do not factor the whims of change into your leadership mindset, you are fooling yourself. Below is a quote from Ray Kurzweil from an article by Chris Meyer in 2003. Ray Kurzweil is an inventor, an entrepreneur, an author, and a futurist. He is the creator of the first reading machine for the blind, speech recognition technology, and many other technologies that help envision the future. He said:

> *We are entering an age of acceleration. The models under-lying society at every level, which are largely based on a linear model of change, are going to have to be redefined. Because of the explosive power of exponential growth, the 21st century will be equivalent to 20,000 years of prog-ress at today's rate of progress; organizations have to be able to redefine themselves at a faster and* faster pace.

All you have to do is look at the business landscape to know this is true. We have technologies and companies in existence today that people would not have thought possible 20 years ago. The power of the computer has produced innovations that science fiction just recently thought were 200 years out. Indeed, we have actual technology today that was previously only available on *The Jetsons* or *Star Trek*!

To see a great example of the exponential change in technology, just look at man's actual space travel. Soon, we will be celebrating the 50th anniversary of man landing on the moon. Do you realize that every time you check your smartphone, you are holding more computer power in the palm of your hand than was present in the spacecraft used to get from the earth to the moon? Pretty awesome when you think of it like that!

With the constant advances in every aspect of our lives, a leader is going to have to deal with change, and should, in fact, look forward to that. When you accept this premise, you then realize that a part of leadership is anticipating change and thinking through how best to manage it. All of the leadership skills and tips we have discussed are still very much a part of this process: Teamwork, properly utilizing your people, looking to your managers for advice, etc. All are very much in play here. An effective leader will focus on these traits and use them to embrace change, to take advantage of new circumstances and new opportunities. Just as I did, you can choose to see the glass as half-full, rather than as half-empty. But you have to want to live in the future, not the past.

Being able to look at change for the opportunities it presents is an attitude. Just like any other leadership trait, it is something that someone can learn and hone with experience. There is an uncomfortable stereotype in business and other walks of life that age is a barometer of how well someone is able to deal with change. The rule of thumb seems to be that the older a person is, the harder it will be for them to deal with change. However, this could not be further from the truth. A person who has been around for some years and is successful is generally proof that they know how to manage change very well. After all, long-term success rarely happens if you cannot adapt to the world. I would argue that in today's fast-paced and ever-changing world, it is impossible to conduct your business the same way day in and day out and still achieve a high level of success.

Leaders who comprehend that they will have to deal with all types of change, and are prepared to be effective when it happens, will go far. An even better leader, though, will study what is going on around her and anticipate the change to take advantage of it. Steve Jobs gives us a prime example. At a time when IBM barely thought about the potential of personal computers, Jobs envisioned bringing one to every home. As a businessman, he had the knack to look at technology's future and marry that to what he believed people would want. Jobs, though, did not only do this with the personal computer. He managed to do this with the iPod, smartphone, and tablet industries. Perhaps his people skills left a great deal to be desired, but who does not wish they bought and hung onto a thousand shares of Apple stock when it first hit the market?

If you are going to excel at leadership, know you must expect to deal with change. Also, be aware that some changes you deal with may occur around the edges. It may not be a direct business situation that throws a monkey wrench into your operations. It may be your health or the health of a loved one that forces you to change. You may have a personal financial setback that affects you. Remember, too, changes are not automatically bad. Perhaps you found that significant other in your life and it means a career reassessment. Maybe you picked the winning ticket in the lottery and now you have things to deal with you only fantasized about in the past (please share with me if you did!). The point is that you need to prepare to be mentally and emotionally tough enough for all of the changes that are going to hit you from every direction in life.

Change occurs in everyone's life. You can either worry about it or you can embrace it. I have learned that change is good. They say that when one door closes, another opens. Sometimes, the new opening may not be obvious. It may only be a window. The important thing is to keep looking for the opportunity that change presents to you.

I hope there are not too many people reading this book who have been shot. It is not a fun experience. However, because of the way I approached this monumental change in my life, I have a richness in my personal and professional life that I would not have experienced in any other way. Because of all that I had to go through, I have a very loving and deep relationship with my wife, Dahlia—you will hear about that later. Believe me, she deserves her own place in this book.

Embrace change as I did. We can certainly allow ourselves moments to feel sorry for ourselves when hit with some negative change in our life. But that negative could turn into something incredibly positive. Life is too long, and life is filled with so many wonderful events to focus solely on the negative. If you are a leader in business, in your community, or in your family, know that you are going to have tons of opportunities heading your way. Some of them may be disguised as an unwanted change. Now, though, you know that they can be much more than that.

KEY TAKEAWAYS

1. You cannot stop change from happening, but you can embrace it and prepare for it.

2. Change is good, and with the right attitude we can all find a way to succeed.

3. You cannot have innovation, progress, or advancements without change.

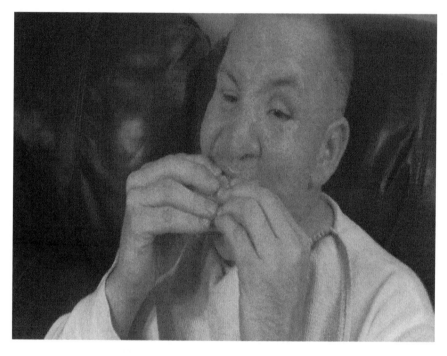

It was six years before my mouth was rebuilt to the point where I could use upper dentures to bite into food. Here, Dahlia made delicious yet tiny sliders that I could actually bite with my new dentures, although due to the scar tissue in my mouth, it would not open up very widely.

We often had to work with the Iraqi Army in our efforts to pay the local Iraqi citizens the money they were due when we made mistakes. I trusted my Marines to handle the situations appropriately, but if anything went wrong that would have been on me.

CHAPTER 9

TAKE RESPONSIBILITY FOR YOUR ACTIONS

ONE OF THE MANY things the United States Marine Corps emphasizes is the importance of doing your job, and doing it well. You can imagine how important this is in a battlefield situation. When all hell is breaking out around you, it is important to know that you can depend on your fellow Marines focusing on their responsibilities. You want to know that your riflemen are returning fire, that the communications specialist is keeping in steady contact with the base command and all elements of your group, that the medical personnel are treating the wounded, etc. As a leader, this comfort allows you to make appropriate decisions in the heat of battle.

Of course, what ties this all together is that the leaders in battle are doing their jobs, too. The people under them need to have that level of trust in leadership, as well, so that they can perform *their* duties. It is a full-blown circle of trust and responsibility. Everyone's functions and tasks are tied together so that everyone can achieve the mission objectives. This is the same principle that should govern your actions in your company or organization. So much of what we have already talked about in this book feeds directly into this principle.

However, there is something that you need to do before you impress this ideal upon your team. You cannot go about encouraging others to focus on their jobs if you are not willing to do the same with your own responsibilities. It is important that you have a clear idea of what your job entails. If you are the head of a company, it is a good idea to actually write down your objectives as the owner or CEO. This is also true of any middle management position, but, in this case, you need to make sure that they are consistent with the objectives of your superiors. Nothing hurts your status as a leader more than working very hard on one thing, only to discover it was not really part of your responsibility!

Having a clear idea of your job's parameters is more important than ever before. No matter the arena, it seems like a problem in too many leadership positions is the amount of additional work thrown on people. As was pointed out earlier, we live in a constantly changing world. This usually means we have more work directed toward us than we originally anticipated. That is going to happen a lot, and a great leader needs to be flexible. However, this same leader is also going to need to do a reality check on a consistent basis to make sure what they are doing is what they should be doing. When your superiors judge—and pay you—to be successful in certain responsibilities, you need to really look to see if the additional work imposed on you is necessary or is, in fact, counterproductive to your stated responsibilities. If unnecessary or counterproductive to your purpose, then you and your bosses need to sit down and discuss this issue. If there is not a clear understanding of what your specific responsibilities and action items are, then what often happens is that you get distracted from working on your primary responsibilities. The funny thing is that it is usually only your chief duties that are part of your quarterly and annual reviews, not all of the other minutia you feel is necessary to focus on daily.

Human nature and corporate culture are such that employees at every level feel compelled to take on whatever is handed to them from above. Therefore, you and your superiors need a clear understanding as to how additional duties will affect your overall job performance. Make sure that you sum up, in writing, any discussions you have. I have heard more than one tale of woe from leaders in middle management where a boss told them something in a conversation that was conveniently, for the boss, forgotten later. After such a discussion, send an email or note clarifying the results of the conversation. It is not so much to make sure your superior sticks to what they say to you, as it is to safeguard that your efforts will not be questioned if that person leaves and you get a new boss.

Sometimes we are so eager to leap into a leadership role that we do not take the time to understand what that role entails. By thinking through these steps to have a clear conception of what you need to be successful as a leader, you are putting yourself in a position to thrive. A map is useless if you cannot figure out where you are in relation to where you want to go. Having a clear job description and goals gives you both the starting point and the final destination for your role in the company.

Once you are comfortable knowing your responsibilities, it is important to focus on them constantly. Too many times, a manager and her boss come up with goals for the year. Then both the boss and manager get busy with running things and shove the goal sheet into a file folder, forgetting it until a week before review time. A leader should avoid this both in himself and in those people he is managing. The same, of course, is true in our personal lives, as well—I need only mention New Year resolutions. I advise people to make a detailed list at the beginning of the year, but to also review them quarterly to see where they stand.

First, let us look at this in terms of your leadership and how such a review process can affect your responsibilities. Part of being a leader is constantly prioritizing your responsibilities, to make the most of what you have at any given point. A common expression in the military is that no battle plan survives enemy contact. No, the enemy always has a say in the matter, and there are simply too many uncontrollable variables to truly plan how things will go down. In Iraq, despite our best efforts and care, we hit IEDs every single day, causing incredible damage to our equipment and to our people. Just as a hundred things can go wrong on the battlefield, so too can a hundred things go wrong at work. How many of us have ended a workday and reflected on the fact that we did not do one thing we set out to do at the beginning of the day? Not one thing that was on the to-do list got done, but we were still busy doing "things." It happens quite often. Bosses, employees, emergencies: Everything has the potential to introduce factors that throw everything off. Without constantly referring back to the main goals of our job and prioritizing them, you can easily get so far behind on key aspects of your responsibilities that it becomes impossible to catch up. It is like a boat that comes loose from its moorings. Unless someone grabs it quickly, it will just drift away with the current and becomes harder and harder to find.

Now we will look at the other side of the coin. You are a manager and have people reporting to you. We will assume you did all of the work with your people so that they have clear job descriptions and specific goals to work on in their roles at work. A good leader will work closely with her people so that they will achieve their goals. First, you want your people to be successful. Second—and this is an obvious point that so many leaders seem to miss—you must make sure your people are successful in their roles to be successful in your own. I knew in Iraq that in order for me to be combat ready every day, submit all my daily reports on time, and provide true value to the battalion commander, my Marines had to do their jobs perfectly for me, as well. I depended on them to do their jobs. It is your responsibility as a leader to encourage your people to follow their job requirements. This means that you have the obligation not to constantly shower them with a bunch of work that is above and beyond their capability to handle. If you cannot avoid handing them additional assignments, then you need to sit down and redefine their job descriptions and goals. You cannot expect your people to be successful if you purposely put them in a situation where success is a paper tiger.

As you can see, this attention to responsibilities ties into the teamwork and communication strengths of leadership we have already discussed. You cannot expect something from the people you lead if they have no idea what that expectation is. This fosters the need for good communication that, in turn, strengthens teamwork. For the most part, people excel at doing their job when they understand what is expected and why it has value. Taking that little bit of extra time to make sure that your team buys into their jobs is often the difference between success and failure.

Now, you are prepared to take responsibility for your role in the company or organization. You know that a significant part of that is being responsible for those who report to you. The most junior leader in the military is responsible for other people, and we take that obligation very seriously. It is also just as relevant in the civilian sector. So, besides your manager changing things on the fly, economic conditions, and a myriad of other issues that you cannot even imagine at this point, what else do you have to worry about?

Mistakes. Your mistakes.

We all make them. We can do something wrong for so many reasons that a list would take up the rest of the book. Whatever the reason, it is a good idea to prepare yourself in advance for how to handle mistakes when they crop up. Any gaffe is going to have its own unique ramifications, but there are two things you should set your mind to do when they occur. One, own up to the mistake. Two, learn from it.

President Harry Truman famously had a plaque on his desk that read, "The buck stops here." He knew that, as president of the United States, any decision by his administration was his responsibility. It did not matter if the secretary of state insulted a foreign dignitary and started a war. It would ultimately be Harry's responsibility. President Truman understood this facet of leadership. Right or wrong, whatever happens under your watch is your responsibility.

Tossing blame around for a mistake like a hot potato does not breed respect. It does not matter where you are: in government, business, or some other organization. We have seen it done so much in the media by public and business figures that everyone recognizes when it is happening. It does not fool anyone. Furthermore, it seems inevitable that when someone is trying to pass the blame for a mistake she made, sooner or later it will fall back on her. At that point, they just look that much worse than if they had simply admitted the screw up in the first place.

You can really hurt yourself in the eyes of your superiors and staff if you try to hide your mistakes. It negatively influences the entire trust paradigm. When you start losing the trust of those above and below you, it will greatly affect your ability to lead. It is especially hard when a person takes on the attitude that a mistake is always someone else's fault. Those above you will have a negative impression of your ability based purely on your passing the buck. Those below you will not feel that you have their back, either, especially if you constantly blame them when things go wrong.

While in Iraq at our base camp, the Sergeant Major issued an order that nobody could park a vehicle behind the chow hall. There were to be no exceptions—if you wanted to use the chow hall, you would have to walk. I passed along this directive to my Marines, but did not think it would be an issue because we typically walked over there anyway. Well, it was only a few days later that a problem arose. My staff sergeant, which is the equivalent of a mid-level manager in the civilian sector, for some reason I still cannot understand, drove one of our vehicles over to the chow hall and parked behind it. Almost as if the scene were scripted, the vehicle (Humvees do not require keys) was confiscated by the sergeant major.

I had been out on one of our combat missions that day, so had no idea about any of this until I got back to our compound late in the day. I did not hear about it from the staff sergeant, which would have helped. Instead, one of my other Marines told me that he was not sure of all the details, but that the staff sergeant was trying to get some of the junior Marines to help him find the vehicle. My staff sergeant was desperately trying to remedy the situation before I got back and caught wind of his mistake. In fact, he did not mention anything about it when I walked past him upon my return. For anybody who has worked in an environment like this, it should be obvious that the leadership element would notify me of the situation right away. They would hold me responsible for having one of my vehicles parked by the chow hall.

My staff sergeant scoured the base for hours, well past nightfall, trying to find and reclaim the vehicle. It was not until late in the evening that he finally came to me and admitted what he had done. The sergeant major had notified me of the incident hours before. As you may predict, I was less upset with him for the actual indiscretion (although that was pretty bad) than I was for all the effort he put into trying to cover up what he had done wrong (and also for including the junior Marines in his attempted cover up). Frankly, I did not look at him the same way after that, and I know the rest of the Marines felt the same way.

It is important that a good leader learn from his mistakes. In Billy Joel's song, *Second Wind*, he says, "You're not the only one who's made mistakes, but they're the only thing that you can truly call your own." This is a truth you have to become comfortable with as a leader. You will make mistakes. Mistakes happen. They happen to everybody and they will happen to you. Mistakes are a badge of leadership. The thing that you must always have to remember is that while mistakes are inevitable, you have to make a point of always learning from them.

In talking about world history, the philosopher George Santayana famously said, "Those who cannot remember the past are condemned to repeat it." You have to make this the motto of your own personal history. When you make a mistake, take into account all of the factors that led to it, determine what you could have done differently and how you may have better utilized personnel, and think about how you can recognize a similar situation in the future. By making this exercise an automatic response to any mistake, you will put yourself in a better position to successfully work through such an issue when it pops up again. We can go through all of the training and simulations in the world, but they never have as much impact as what we learn from a real world situation where we made a bad decision. They are the lessons that last.

I can summarize this chapter by saying that you need to take ownership of your position at work. Whenever we own something, we treat it much better than if we borrow or rent it. A home is a perfect example. If you rent an apartment or house, you will keep it clean and nice, but any major work is up to the landlord. You do not see any reason to put a great deal of time or money into the place. When you own your house, however, you treat it differently. You take extra pains to make it exactly as you want it. You take care of any repairs quickly so that a minor issue does not lead to more serious problems. You invest in your home, emotionally as well as financially, as completely as you can.

That is exactly how you have to treat your leadership position at work. You have to make it your own. Doing so will give you the best chance for success. In addition, one of your jobs as a leader is to teach this same sense of ownership to all of the people who work for you. When you and your people have that sense of commitment to what you do, you are going to operate as a well-coordinated organization. That is how I learned things in the military. Marines learn that whatever job they have is important, and that they need to do their best at it. Everyone depends on everyone doing his job. If you have a thousand people buying into that same concept, then together you can move mountains. However many people report to you, it is your responsibility—and it is to your benefit—to inspire this sense of ownership in them.

We talked about some heavy issues in this chapter. Indeed, the lessons of leadership throughout this book are serious. However, this does not mean that a leader cannot have a sense of humor. Leadership can get stressful. So I want to remind you how important it is to maintain a good sense of humor. As an example, not long after I got to the hospital and was recovering from being shot—and, remember, I deployed with an infantry battalion and not as a lawyer—my dad sat down next to me and reminded me of the universal feeling toward attorneys. He said to me, "See, Justin, even in Iraq they know who the lawyers are!" Thanks, Dad.

I have to love my dad. He could see everything I was going through, and it had to hurt him to watch me. But he knew that throwing a little joke in like that helped to ease the tension we both felt. I have carried this lesson with me over my road of recovery and into the work I do now. When you are a leader, people look to you to set the tone for whatever the job you and they are tasked with, be it running a department, a division, or the entire company. That aspect of leadership is as important for you to know as understanding the actual technical requirements necessary to do your job. If your people see that you are calm and able to crack a joke when things get tense, then they are more likely to respond in kind to stressful situations. Remember, you are a role model. You are always setting the example.

KEY TAKEAWAYS

1. Do not hold your people accountable for criteria that is outside their area of responsibility.

2. Take responsibility for your mistakes, and then learn from them.

3. A sense of humor can go a long way when used appropriately.

Here is one of Lieutenant Colonel Desgrosseilliers' Marines providing "guardian angel" over-watch during one of our missions. This Marine had a very focused responsibility that day and took it very seriously.

Investing in your people can include your team at work, a particular organization that you support or any other group. I have supported a wide variety of wounded warrior organizations over the years.

CHAPTER 10

BE A TEACHER AND MENTOR

NO MATTER THE BUSINESS or organization, I cannot stress enough the two-fold responsibility of every leader: You are responsible up, and you are responsible down. You are responsible to your manager or superior to meet your goals and objectives. Likewise, you have a responsibility to those who report to you to ensure that they can be successful in their jobs. In a very good company, this role of leadership permeates all levels of the organization so that everyone works for the benefit of those above and below their position. If this has not been a part of your corporate culture, then you should be the one to start it!

If you have never been in the military, then you may not realize that teaching is very much a part of its "corporate philosophy." In the Marines, teaching is the constant theme of everything we do. Yes, you have instructors initially teaching you the basic fundamentals of using weapons, physical fitness, and how to work as a unit. Through-out your career in the Marines, though, the teaching never stops. As you specialize in a certain discipline, the Marines emphasize that you be the best in your particular skill. In addition, as we stay in the Marine Corps, we attend a variety of schools and academies designed to make us better leaders. Some examples include the Corporals' and Sergeants' Courses, the Staff Noncommissioned Officer Academy, the Expeditionary Warfare School, and the Command and Staff College. A critical part of the curriculum at these institutions is focused on fostering these same leadership ideals in those under you.

While a great deal of training and instruction is in a classroom setting, probably the most important training I received in the Marines was by seeing the examples of others and experiencing the personal attention I received from superiors. This was true from my first boss in Okinawa, Japan, to Lieutenant Colonel Desgrosseilliers in Habbaniyah, Iraq. They had a vested interest in my being the best Marine and officer I could be. They knew it would be important not only to me, but also to their own commands and to the Corps as a whole. This is the same philosophy you need as a leader in your company or organization.

Poor leaders look at training, or taking the time to teach, as a drain on their time and resources. That outlook is incredibly shortsighted and, unfortunately, all too common. Some leaders figure that people who work for them should simply know their jobs; otherwise, they would not be there in the first place. This is one of the biggest fallacies in business today, and one that leads to many problems. When you take a leadership position, never assume. If you are promoted to a group that you have never worked with, then you must take the time to evaluate what your people know. You could very well be walking into a situation where your predecessor did a terrible job at training the group. They may be doing everything wrong! If you do not take the time to evaluate your personnel, then you will be doing them a disservice if you assign them a task that they are not ready to do. In a similar vein, you may be walking into a situation where those below you are so effective that you can learn a great deal from them. You cannot effectively lead if you do not know the strengths and weaknesses of your people. Only by taking the time to assess the individuals that compose your new group will you know what additional training you need to provide for them.

As a leader, there are two types of training you can provide. One is formal classroom and group training. The second type is the individual work you can do with members of your staff. Let us take a brief look at the first form of training.

Companies should provide training that will help the employees become better and succeed at their jobs. This type of training can run the gamut from trainings in very specific disciplines all the way to general managerial training. This training can be conducted by in-house people or the company may have brought in an outside consultant. The training can also take the form of conferences that employees can attend. The concept, here, is to give an employee the opportunity to learn from experts and the chance to interact with her peers. Formal training is a great way for a person to learn her job and to prepare her for more responsibility in the future.

I owe my life to people being properly trained in their jobs. The most obvious people are George, and I already explained to you that he had received training for that type of surgery on a pig, and my many doctors, especially those at the forward surgical unit. Lt. Col. Desgrosseilliers was a huge part of that as well, of course. Based on his training and experience, he knew exactly how to react and how to align the rest of the Marines and vehicles to protect me. In turn, each one of those Marines knew exactly what they were supposed to do to establish the defensive perimeter, looking outward and scanning for any sign of the sniper, that allowed George the time to get me ready for the Humvee ride. Everyone on our team and in every team that dealt with me had received extensive training in their professions—and it paid off when I needed it the most.

Unfortunately, many companies and organizations cut back on training opportunities when there is a cash crunch or whenever trimming the budget becomes a priority. When this occurs, you owe it to your team to try to reinstate or increase training. We have talked a great deal in this book about teamwork and trust. But nothing helps develop these traits more than when everybody on the team understands the importance of and how to perform their jobs. When this is the sense across all members of the group, it is easier for people to rely on one another. On a personal level, there is a wonderful feeling when you realize you truly know your job. When someone gets to this level of comfort with what they are doing, it offers more opportunities for that individual to exceed expectations and contribute more to the group. Your confidence in your competence will show through. Your actions are then speaking louder than your words—always a good thing for someone in a leadership role.

It is very important for a leader to provide formal training experiences for his people. As we have seen, these are crucial for the success of any organization, but a great leader needs to step up to the plate and do more. This is where managers understand that they are always teaching their employees, too. A good leader needs to take the time to work with her staff whenever the opportunity presents itself. Some people try to avoid these "teachable moments" as cliché, but an enlightened leader will pounce on them at every opportunity.

As a leader, you need to look at these chances as a way to strengthen your people and your ability to meet goals. Your employees are going to become more comfortable in doing their jobs well with formal training. When you help them achieve increased proficiency in their roles, your employees are going to hold you in higher regard as their manager. They will know that they can come to you with a problem and that you will help them find a solution for the issue. You may not only be teaching them a certain skill, but you are promoting better communication, trust, and teamwork among your people at the same time.

As a manager, you should also know who in your department you can trust with certain tasks. By working one-on-one with individuals when needed, you will have firsthand knowledge of what each can do. This allows you to use better judgment when assigning your personnel to certain duties—it allows you to more effectively use the strengths of the team where they are needed. By getting to know your staff through teaching opportunities, you recognize that one may be better at overall organizational skills while another excels at making accurate projections. You will know if you have a member of your team who can lead others, but you may not want them near any paperwork. Understanding your people can only happen through close interaction with them. That is why recognizing and seizing on teachable moments can add so much value when building your team.

In any discussion about leadership, you need to know that a great leader puts her employees' needs first and empowers them to perform at their highest levels. Being good in the workplace is usually a combination of formal schooling, experience, and the practical advice of mentors at work. Such a combination gives a company well-rounded employees who will be successful and, by their efforts, make the company successful. This same principle breaks down into each department of the business. Whether you are the CEO or the manager of an individual division, putting yourself out there to mentor and teach your staff will pay off in huge dividends to everyone involved.

Remember that there are countless ways of teaching a member of your staff. Sometimes, you need to bring a person in and systematically explain something they did wrong, telling them the steps they have to take to fix it. Other times, somebody is going to come in with a question or a problem. It is important to really listen to what is being said. This way, you can try to center on the crux of the matter and guide your employee to the best solution.

One of the ways I remember learning in the Marines is that my trainers would tell us stories to illustrate a certain point. In the Marine Corps, all the officers go through six months of training at Quantico to learn how to be rifle platoon commanders. As part of that instruction, the trainers periodically related to us inspirational stories of amazing bravery and valor displayed by other Marines in war. Not only did these stories honor the individuals talked about, but they also inspired us to strive and emulate them when we thought we had reached our limits. In fact, I read one of those stories about an incredible Medal of Honor recipient to our unit right before we deployed. Most people remember a story before they remember the nuts and bolts of how to do something. Do not be afraid to illustrate your teaching moments with stories from your own experience. Not only will it have a lasting impact on the person you are teaching, but it will also help build that personal connection that you want to have with your people.

You are always going to find people working for you who are

exceptional. They have the skills and talent to take them a long way in their profession. This is where you may want to take this person under your wing and serve as their mentor. Mentoring is a personal developmental relationship in which a more experienced or knowledgeable person helps to guide a less experienced or knowledgeable person. The mentor can be older or younger, but has developed a certain area of expertise. It is a learning partnership between someone with vast experience and someone who wants to learn.

Obviously, this is more involved than simply being a leader who does a good job at teaching her staff. It takes more time, and the mentor's goal is to help broaden the overall talents of the particular person he is working with—the focus, here, is not on the team, but on the individual. I think everyone can think back and can pick out those one or two people who made a huge impact on their life. It could be a parent, teacher, boss, coach, commanding officer, etc. The point is that one person probably influenced you in many ways that helped make you the person you are today. Whether they made a conscious decision or not, that influential person was one of your mentors.

Keep in mind that good leadership means developing the talents of those working for you. When you go that extra step and act as a mentor, you are fulfilling one of your biggest responsibilities. As you help a member of your staff get better at their job, it will make the goals and objectives of your position easier to achieve. Not only are you helping that person to become successful, but you are also helping the rest of your team by advancing the team's collective skill set. I hope that one of your goals as a leader is to help others to rise and take on their own leadership roles.

Unfortunately, there are leaders who shy away from taking on meaningful mentoring roles with their people. It is not that they are unable to do it; rather, it is that they are afraid that the person they mentor will rise above them. You can see that all of the leadership skills in this book are intertwined. Here, we have that problem of arrogance and self-doubt creeping into the equation. If a leader is afraid of having one of her own people surpass him, then they should not be in a leadership position in the first place.

In one of the old *Honeymooner* episodes, Ralph (Jackie Gleason) is telling Norton (Art Carney) that he follows the adage, "Be kind to the people you meet on the way up, because you're going to meet the same people on the way down." We all have aspirations in our professional lives. You can work hard, but maybe you are never going to quite get to the pinnacle that you would like. This happens often—there simply may not be enough leadership roles to accommodate everyone. A manager often finds that he is working for someone he originally trained when he was that person's supervisor. Would you want to work for a person who fondly remembers you as one of his mentors at an important point in his life? I would. You should be mentoring good people as a part of your job, but remember that this circumstance could very well happen to you. It just makes you a better person, generally, to use your leadership position to further the careers of those in your charge.

You are not building your team and promoting trust if you are afraid of people who work for you. By this, I mean that if you are anxious about the knowledge and talents of your subordinates outshining you, then you will be outshone sooner rather than later. It is more important to some managers that others see them as the one with all of the answers. These are the ones who inevitably fail to reach their own personal goals of leadership in a company. Remember, you have to check your ego at the door. I know of one man who thought of himself as the smartest person in the room. He started his own company. He tried hard to hire the best people available, but then did not listen to their counsel and advice as he navigated the minefield of a start-up company. The short version of his story is that the company never started up. Much of the failure had to do with his inability or fear of using the talents of the people around him.

In the Marines and other branches of the military, it is a point of pride that the men and women under you get the opportunity to blossom and advance in their careers. We make a big production when it comes to promotions or special recognition. In sports, you often hear of "coaching trees." This is where you can trace the successful careers of many coaches to one coach that they all started out under. It is a point of pride with the original coach to take some credit for all of the fruitful careers he fostered. The same should be true for you in whatever business or organization you work.

Having your people receive a promotion should not be a threat or a source of fear to a good manager. Rather, it should be one of the explicit goals of the manager's job—to make those for whom he is responsible shine in the organization. Like everything else you do as a leader, promotions for your people do not happen by accident. You have to make it a priority to have training sessions available to your people and get them to attend. In addition to that, you have to make the effort to step in and do the personal teaching and mentoring whenever possible. This does take work on your part, and it is not something that comes naturally to all managers. It may be one of those skills that a leader consciously has to learn—and learn to act on—when the opportunity presents itself.

The ironic thing about being a good leader is that when you do take the time for teaching, you are actually making more work for yourself. If you are very good at doing this, your people are going to get promoted out from under you. This means you will have new personnel coming in that you have to train up. It can be a never-ending circle. That does not mean it is a bad thing, however. You must recognize that your leaders are identifying your talents in this regard. It may be your training skills that are most valued as a great leader. Your own recognitions and promotions will come with time because your bosses see the wonderful success you have with your staff, over and over again as you train them to lead themselves. There is no greater win-win situation than when you take the time to work closely with those under your supervision. Done correctly, the company is going to thrive, your people will be recognized and advance—and so will you.

KEY TAKEAWAYS

1. Investing in your people not only increases productivity but also demonstrates that you care about them.

2. Getting to know your people is critical to a well-functioning team—not only will you be able to deploy them in the most effective manner, but mutual trust will develop over time.

3. Personal mentorship is often lacking in today's businesses—do not let that happen with you!

I am extremely fortunate to now be in a position to mentor George Grant, who saved my life in Iraq. One good turn deserves another!

Although I previously served as a trial attorney, for the first three moths of my recovery the doctors were not sure if I would speak again. Now, speaking clearly is a real challenge due to the damage to my mouth and tongue, but I conquered my fear of failure by practicing and practicing and practicing. I now speak in front of tens of thousands of people every year.

CHAPTER 11

CONQUER YOUR OWN FEARS

AS YOU HAVE SEEN throughout this book, many components make up a successful leader. It is always important to remember that few people are "natural born leaders." The majority of people who find themselves in a leadership role need actually to learn many of the concepts that we have talked about in this book. This is true in the military, and certainly in business. Chairman of the Joint Chiefs of Staff Martin Dempsey has said, "Leaders are readers." This is about developing yourself as a leader. The abilities to adapt, embrace change, to see change before it washes over you, and to make very tough decisions all require you to continue developing yourself and to be a lifelong learner. Even great leaders have to go through periods of working on leadership skills they lack. In fact, I believe the definition of a good leader is one who realizes her deficiencies, but takes the steps to overcome those issues.

You can see this all of the time in the Marines. Officers and staff non-commissioned officers achieve their rank through hard work and persistence. They attend the required training and get everything they can out of those courses. They watch and learn from their peers and superiors. Most importantly, they learn from their experiences and occasional mistakes. Good, strong leaders view mistakes as experiences for learning and growth; weaker people often perceive mistakes as evidence that they are failures. These strong leaders often spend extra time on areas of leadership where they are weak.

The biggest obstacle for any leader to overcome is when one of their weaknesses is actually a fear. Not everybody is very good at dealing with her fears. For instance, we have talked, here, about how good communication with your subordinates is so important to building teamwork and meeting your group's goals. Many people have trouble with this practice. They would rather do anything than sit down and get to know their people better. Some tend to be much more comfortable sending out emails and encouraging other forms of electronic communication. I have met leaders who do everything by text message! That may avoid the problem for a time, but it is going to greatly handicap someone in a leadership position if they hope to sustain any kind of success.

There are many personal and psychological reasons that a person cannot face their fears. Books and college courses are devoted to the subject. We cannot adequately cover all of that material here, but I can give you some practical insight into what you can do if you have trouble with a fear that is handicapping your abilities as a leader.

First of all, you need to know that you have a fear that you need to work on. I guess this can be compared to an addict needing to admit that they have a problem before they can successfully deal with it. They have to say, "I am an alcoholic," or "I am a drug addict," or whatever it may be to start the process. Perhaps you received a promotion into a leadership position because you did your job very well. But perhaps in that job, you never had to deal with people as you do now as their leader. These new responsibilities can be intimidating and may keep you up at night. You have to realize that there are elements to this new position that you are afraid of, and that this is something you will have to figure out how to overcome.

The one thing you do not want to do is to hide that fear. Some people will do whatever they can to mask their fears; the fact is that good managers and leaders work on overcoming them. Besides, history is full of examples where the cover-up always makes any type of situation worse. President Nixon is usually the poster boy for this type of behavior gone wrong. You can only get by for so long by avoiding your biggest sources of frustration. Remember, nobody has the answers for everything. If you really want to be an exceptional leader, you will look at situations where you are lacking skills as your opportunity to improve and get that much better at your job. Besides, one of the best feelings in the world is when we can overcome a personal difficulty—not hide from it or sweep it under the rug, but take the necessary steps to turn a liability into an asset.

I want to give you an example of this very issue from my own life, from when I was really coming to terms with the fact that I was on a long and difficult road to recovery. Besides all the physical difficulties and surgeries I had to face, I needed to deal with the fact that I also had PTS. This is something you constantly hear about in the news today, but it is very difficult to fully grasp until you go through it. Ironically, due to media stories and Hollywood movies, the American public typically identifies PTS with war veterans. Actually, the vast majority of those across our country who face PTS are civilians who have been victims of rape or other violent assault, have been in car crashes and natural disasters, or have grown up in extremely challenging communities.

Of course, there is a technical, medical definition of PTS, but I think it is easier to really define it using everyday language. PTS can occur after you have been through a trauma. A trauma is a shocking event that you witness or that actually happens to you. During such an event, you think that your life, or another person's life, is in danger. You may feel afraid or think that you have no control over what is happening.

I assume my PTS is from when I was shot. However, it could easily have been caused just by being in a war zone, by almost being blown up two weeks before I was shot, or from participating in memorial services for Marines I will never see again. Although my symptoms and triggers are similar to many others, everyone is a little bit different. Like many others who experience PTS, I no longer like being in crowds, loud noises are a big problem for me, I stay inside on the Fourth of July, and I have a really tough time watching most war movies. Eight years have now passed since I was injured—and I still face recurring nightmares and am hyper-vigilant. I have never had suicidal ideas or thought about hurting others, but those are also common symptoms.

When my wife and I first identified that I had PTS, it was difficult for me to wrap my head around that and to ask for the help that I needed. But I figured I had two choices. On the one hand, I could handle this the healthy way and talk to a professional who had worked with other warriors before and who could help explain why my mind and body were reacting this way. Maybe he could explain why I would randomly start crying if I saw a young man in uniform, why I constantly scanned the roads for bombs as if I were back in Iraq, and why I felt so undeserving of having survived when so many others did not. On the other hand, I could keep my problems bottled up inside and just see what would happen. I decided to seek help from a professional and to learn what was going on with me.

I discovered that learning about a fear goes a long way in helping to overcome it. For one thing, the big reason for many "fears" is not having enough information about them. It is natural to fear the unknown. In my research, I discovered that PTS has been around for as long as there have been wars. We know from letters written home by soldiers in our Civil War that many soldiers on both sides suffered greatly from the stresses of military life. At the time, the medical profession referred to PTS as "Soldier's Heart" and "Exhausted Heart." Of the 15,027 Union Army soldier health records examined in one study, 44 percent reported signs of nervous disease after the war. Since the Civil War, PTS has also been referred to as Shell Shock, Combat Fatigue, and Battle Stress.

In fact, descriptions of PTS go back thousands of years to Greek and Roman times. Did you ever have to read Homer's *The Odyssey* when you were in high school or college? We had to read it in my high school, but it was not until I went back and looked at it again as an adult that I truly understood it. It actually describes an emotional tale of PTS where Odysseus spent several years wandering, drifting around after fighting the Trojan War. He had been through traumatic battle experiences and suffering similar to that which many in today's military have experienced—even though it was 27 centuries ago. Today's doctors would say that much of what Homer described falls under the category of survivor's guilt, flashbacks, loss of interest in work or activities, and depression.

The Greek historian Herodotus wrote a lot about PTS. He talked about one soldier who fought in the battle of Marathon in 490 BC. This soldier went blind after the man standing next to him was killed, even though the blinded soldier "was wounded in no part of his body." Herodotus also wrote about the Spartan leader Leonidas, whom we all now know from the movie *300*. At one point, he dismissed his men from combat because he realized they were mentally exhausted from too much fighting.

As I mentioned earlier, do not for a moment think that military personnel are the only ones to experience PTS. It affects people from all walks of life. Even Charles Dickens wrote about PTS, showing how it could touch anyone. At about the same time as our Civil War, Dickens was involved in a traumatizing railway accident in England in which the front of the train plunged off a bridge that was under repair. Ten people died, another 49 were injured. Dickens wrote, "I begin to feel it more in my head. I sleep well and eat well; but I write half a dozen notes, and turn faint and sick . . . . I am getting right, though still low in pulse and very nervous." After that experience, he was unable to travel by rail. He did not write as much as before the accident, and he actually died on the fifth anniversary of the train crash.

This may be more than you wanted to know about PTS, but facing this fear in my life illustrates a good and healthy way to face any fear that you have. And my learning about the disorder and those that have suffered through it helped me to cope and then overcome. Not only has learning about and asking for help on this very personal issue helped me individually, but because of my knowledge of the disorder and personal experience with it, I have been invited by the Veterans Administration, the Marine Corps, the Wounded Warrior Project, and other groups to talk publicly about PTS in an effort to help others who have to face the demons alone. I am humbled that I was able to turn a very real fear around into something positive, into a way to help so many others. I am happy that I was able to change what I was once so scared of into an asset in my fight. I really enjoy helping other veterans, and that opportunity only presented because, at some point, I decided that I needed to deal with my fear and looked for help. Imagine that you are a young Marine or soldier with PTS. Would you feel more comfortable talking with one of your bosses about issues you may be facing if you heard him talking openly about his experiences with PTS?

You are going to run into all kinds of fears—in fact, you are likely to identify your fears—as you work toward becoming a good leader and moving further up the ladder. As I did with PTS, you need to confront and deal with those fears. It does not matter what others think of them. We have all run into people whose reaction to something they cannot relate to is that it is "no big deal" and to "get over it." If something is holding you back from reaching your full potential, though, it is a big deal. You owe it to yourself, and to your people, to do what you can to address your fears.

The fear leading many top 10 lists is the fear of public speaking. Many people are forced to deal with this fear at some time in their life—in school, at work, in a PTA meeting. But they are often afraid they will make a mistake, that they do not have the requisite knowledge, or that they will not be prepared enough. When you are a manager or hold some other leadership position, public speaking fears quickly become significant as so many of these leadership roles involve giving speeches, presentations, or training sessions to large groups. If you do not do something to overcome this fear, you may find your career path effectively stalled.

I can illustrate for you a practical story of two women who faced this common anxiety, how they addressed it, and what it meant to their careers. Both women worked in the pharmaceutical industry and had high middle-management positions. The first woman worked in the area of hammering out contracts for her company's agreements with different manufacturers and distributors. She did her job well and asked to speak at a conference. She was to give a presentation to the 200 or so people who were there and explain how she did her job. She prepared well, but she was not used to speaking like this. It was a disaster. She swore she would never do anything like that again, and she kept her word. While she continued to do a good job in her role, her company never offered any substantial promotion opportunities to her and she stayed in the same position for years.

The other woman ran into the same situation. In her case, she worked on the compliance side of the industry, also spoke at a conference, and also experienced a small disaster. However, her attitude to the situation was different. She knew how much public speaking could affect her career, and she took steps to improve. She enrolled in public speaking courses offered by her local college. She took every opportunity to speak in front of a group and put her new lessons to practical use. She not only put her lessons into practice at work, but she made herself get up in front of people at church, her kids' school, and some organizations where she volunteered. She even joined the local chapter of Toastmasters to refine her speaking skills. She says that public speaking is still not her favorite thing to do, but you would never know that by listening to her. She has flown up the corporate ladder and she attributes a lot of her mobility to her decision to turn her biggest fear around.

I hope that you receive coaching and encouragement from your supervisor when facing one of your fears. Whether you do or not, remember that this is one of your roles as a leader to those under and around you. A good leader must, of course, know the strengths and weaknesses of everyone on his staff. A great leader, though, will help a staff member work on those weaknesses. This may mean finding appropriate training for a person to attend, pairing a worker up with someone who can help them overcome their issue, or just talking and brainstorming with an employee about the help they need for their own particular issues. This constant thread should run through a manager's day. You have to know your people so that you can help them achieve success in a way that works for their particular skills. This idea is so critical to effective leadership that, in the Marine Corps, one of the criteria upon which we are judged for promotion is the development of our subordinates.

Unfortunately, some managers only talk to their people about the issues that cause problems when they are conducting a formal quarterly or annual review. A leader who conducts his responsibilities in this way is doing a disservice to everyone: himself, his people, and his company. By exercising constant communication, a good leader always has a finger on the pulse of his department. This all comes back to promoting teamwork. Everybody in the group should know that someone has their back. This kind of support goes a long way in getting the team to deal with their own particular fears. Overcoming fear is so much easier when a person knows they are not alone.

Good leaders know that everyone is a constant work in progress, including themselves. We can all learn *some* skills easily, but others may take a lot of work. These tougher ones usually have some aspect of fear that a person needs to face. Like most problems, when you understand this aspect of yourself or in those who report to you, you have made the first meaningful step in turning that fear into an asset. When you recognize your fears in yourself and your people, then you can prepare a course of action to surmount them. By doing this in a consistent fashion in your role as a leader, you share the glory of success with everyone who works with you.

Some braggarts may say, "I don't know the meaning of the word 'fear.'" A successful leader not only knows the meaning of fear, but also knows how to confront it. He can then either eliminate it as a fear, or learn how to work with it. Most importantly, he can also help those who work for him to do the same thing. Was I scared in Iraq when we went out into contested territory on our patrols? Of course. But our team had practiced hour after hour, so we knew exactly how to react when dangerous issues inevitably arose. Addressing those fears by training to confront them head-on allowed us to stay calm and collected under very trying circumstances. Each of you can successfully confront and learn from your own fears in the same way.

KEY TAKEAWAYS

1. Everyone has fears and worries, but not everybody is emotionally mature enough to acknowledge that and turn them around.

2. When someone identifies a fear to you, recognize the strength they displayed in doing so.

3. Developing your team is a continuous effort that requires constant attention.

Mentors come in many forms. I have learned a lot about life and a positive outlook from Leo Thorsness, Medal of Honor recipient and retired Air Force colonel. His six years as a Prisoner of War at the "Hanoi Hilton" in Vietnam make my challenges look like a walk in the park.

After facing a incredibly humbling experience, I will never forget how lucky I am to still be here, and that is primarily due to the heroic efforts of this young Navy Corpsman. Dahlia and I were very excited to welcome him and the rest of Third Battalion, Second Marines home in 2007 at Camp Lejeune, North Carolina.

CHAPTER 12

HUMILITY AND SELF-CONFIDENCE
GO HAND IN HAND

I KNOW I WILL always have problems eating, drinking, communicating, and just remembering for the rest of my life. But I have learned that through inner strength, humility, and a victorious spirit, I can overcome the toughest obstacles. Eight years ago, with my speech impediment and traumatic brain injury, I never would have imagined I would be in front of various groups and corporate America giving inspirational speeches on leadership and other subjects. So just imagine what each of you and your teams are capable of doing when you truly put your mind to it.

While I would love to go back in time and not be in the line of fire when the sniper shot me in the head, it did shape the life I have now. Through the countless and constant efforts of Marines and a Navy corpsman on the battlefield, numerous medical personnel, and all of my friends and family, I am able to live a fulfilling life and, hopefully, serve as a role model to others, inspiring them—and you—to overcome difficulties and succeed.

I do not say any of that lightly. Nor do I say it as a way of patting myself on the back. I am at this place in my life because of the support of others, but in conjunction with my own determination and effort. When I am up in front of a crowd, I am always humbled to be in that position. I do not take it for granted. By any odds maker, my life should have ended in Iraq. I am grateful for each day that I can continue my work, and I never lose sight of all the support I have received that has gotten me to this point.

The same should be true of whatever role you have in your company. Whether you are the CEO of a Fortune 500 company, starting your own business, or working hard as a mid-level manager, you are there on the shoulders of others. It may have been teachers, family, employees, your current team, etc., but the truth is that nobody gets to where they are alone. A failure to recognize this will inevitably result in a rude awakening at some point in a person's professional or personal life (or both).

We all enjoy recognition for a job well done. It may be a special award you receive or a promotion. The same was true in the Marines—I always enjoyed the promotion ceremonies for the opportunity to hear about a Marine's individual accomplishments, and, certainly, those promoted were very excited to embrace their new rank. When this happens, enjoy the moment, but do not let it go to your head. I hope that you thank all the people who contributed to that achievement because the odds are good that you did not do it alone.

When you think about it, recognition and making mistakes are two sides of the same coin—at least in terms of how you should handle them. When you receive recognition or a promotion for your accomplishments, do the following, in the following order: enjoy the moment, realize what you did to get to that point, do not dwell on it, and move on. When you make mistakes, you are not going to enjoy realizing you made a mistake, but make sure you stop for a moment to understand what you did to get to that point, learn from it, do not dwell on it, and move on.

When we do well in a given situation, it generally builds our self-confidence. Recognition of any type feeds our confidence. It usually empowers us to continue to move forward in what we are doing to achieve even greater success. Therefore, remember how the recognition motivated you, and apply that to the people you manage. Sometimes, a simple pat on the back and saying, "Good job," to one of your people will have more influence than any pay raise or formal award ceremony. If you have worked hard to build your team, if they look up to you, then simple recognition and encouragement by you will take your group to the heights that you want to reach.

Often, an appropriate response to a workplace accolade is to say, "I had an awful lot of help," or a simple, "Thank you." Giving such a response sets you up for success in your leadership position. If you are sincere in that response, you are set up to navigate leadership in the proper way. You also avoid turning people off with some false statement that others can immediately see through. Being truly humble in your endeavors increases the respect that those above and below will have for you. It also casts you in a good light in the eyes of your peers. True leadership is about building positives, one on top of another, and empowering others, not hogging the spotlight and self-promoting.

Remember that there is only a razor's edge of difference between arrogance and self-confidence. People can see when you know what you are doing, but that success has not gone to your head. They respect that and want to work with such a person: As a moth streaks toward light, so too will people flock to your leadership if you are humble and build up others—and find success through that. An arrogant person, though, constantly tells others how great he is at his job (whether that is true or not), never seeks the advice of others, and is probably trying to compensate for some sort of shortcoming. The only reason people flock to this person is to see him fall (or get pushed) off his pedestal!

Much of this goes back to the lessons about how important it is to work *with* your people. Never be afraid to roll up your sleeves and plunge into real work with your team. I was a major in Iraq, but that did not mean I did not pick up a broom and help my men clean a warehouse if that was our job. Pitching in where needed and keeping your people's needs first is a great way to stay humble in your leadership role. During our basic officer training, we all learned that taking care of our troops was our number one priority. As a criminal prosecutor in the Marines, I obviously worked in an administrative capacity, but I still took my leadership responsibilities very seriously. I remember when I was the Officer of the Day and I told our sergeant that I wanted to swing by the enlisted barracks to see how our troops were living. I wanted a chance to talk with them outside of the office. To be honest, I was not sure how he would receive my suggestion. But I could tell our sergeant was proud to take me around and show me how squared all of his Marines were and that everything they needed was taken care of. I originally planned to spend an hour there, but returned to my office after three hours. I got to know them a little better than I ever could in our office. It was definitely time well spent for the Marines and me.

You just never know when something you do is going to have a profound impact on someone who is lower in the "pecking order" than you. I recently had a reminder of this from a Marine I encountered in Iraq. He wrote to me about an event that I clearly remember, but had no idea anybody else ever took note of. The note was incredibly touching to me, and helps illustrate my point of not knowing how your actions can affect another. It was from a young Marine named Adam Hart:

> *I was in the 3/2 India Company, 1st Platoon. I was on the 611 bridge in Habbaniyah. I'm not sure if you remember this, but at the time I was a corporal and our squad went out on a patrol with you around the area. On the way back in to the base, I got stuck in some C-wire.[1] I started to panic and tugged at my pants leg to break free because two guys were shot right in that area by a sniper in the past few weeks. I was a sitting duck, so to speak. Tugging my leg made the situation worse and I was not accomplishing anything. But then you came up and shielded me with your body toward the city. You told me to calm down and relax and that you would help me get out.*
>
> *In that situation, you made me feel at ease and I felt safe.*

---

1   C-Wire is a common abbreviation for concertina wire. It is rolled coils of barbed wire that we often unrolled as part of defense measures around our operating bases. Unfortunately, it is very easy to get yourself caught in that wire when you attempt to cross through it.

At the time, I couldn't believe a Major would put his life out there to help me. The next day on the bridge, I woke up in the afternoon after standing post, and I heard that you got shot in the head. It crushed me inside because I assumed that you passed on. I kept thinking about the day before and what you did for me. Anything could have happened in that situation, but you took that risk. That action you did really impacted me. To this day I would tell people how you did that for me and that unfortunately you got killed the next day (luckily I get to change the ending now).

About 6 months ago, I was reading about wounded warriors and I came across your story. After I read it, I couldn't believe that it was you and you were alive. After all these years of thinking about it and talking about it, knowing that you were alive was a feeling I couldn't express. And seeing what you have done and accomplished since then is amazing and an inspiration. I would like to say thank you and that it is really good to see that you are doing well. Hope this finds you well.

Semper Fi!

Receiving that letter was stunning, to say the least. In fact, I do not know the right words to express how I felt when I first read it, but it did make me start crying. I am not sure why—the letter is nothing but optimistic and everything worked out well. But Adam's words eight years later had a huge impact on me, and apparently my actions had a big impact on him as well. To have that type of influence on someone is a big responsibility. I am honored that Adam remembered my actions and I am sure it influenced how he worked with others during his deployment. Semper Fi!

Every now and then we all need reminders that we are doing the right thing. When someone tells you of the influence you had on them, it is worth all the promotions and awards in the world.

Humility means understanding that you are always there for your people, not for yourself. Remember that Harry Truman's desk held the plaque that said, "The buck stops here." Well, truly responsible leaders do not make excuses when things go wrong. Good leaders do not blame others. They save their energy, deal, and focus on the future. Leaders stay calm, cool, and collected. Leaders think about what to do, not what has happened. They focus on the opportunities of tomorrow rather than the problems or accolades of yesterday. A leader who has achieved this correct balance of humility and confidence can successfully advance his objectives, the organization's goals, and his career.

My injury was some time ago, now, but I am still recovering and have more surgeries in my future. I have had plenty of time to think about personal responsibility, goals, and the definition of success. I have come to realize that no matter what hand life may deal, we alone are ultimately responsible for the quality of our lives. If we want to improve any area of our lives, whether we wish to have more money, more success, more happiness, or more love, it is up to us to institute the changes necessary to make that happen. I decide what is important to me, what my short and long-term goals in my personal and professional lives are, and how I am going to achieve them.

As you focus on and advance in your own leadership role, you will continue to grow. You will find that keeping your confidence and humility in perspective will help you handle the additional responsibility that you will inevitably acquire. Your growing confidence will help you take decisive action, while your humility will keep you working with your subordinates and continue to help them succeed—the key to making sure you keep advancing along the right track.

By now, I hope you realize that being a strong leader means you have to work proactively with those who answer to you. An important component of leadership is your vision. As a leader, developing your vision, clearly articulating it, and then disseminating it through a number of different channels is critical. Included within that is setting realistic, demanding goals and then going after them relentlessly, with the help of other talented men and women who are equally as committed and engaged. Your confidence will fuel your ability to do these things; your humility will never allow you to forget how to treat those members of your team or department.

Leaders always move forward, face danger and uncertainty, and take risks even when there is no guarantee of success. As J.R.R. Tolkien wrote in *The Lord of the Rings*, "It's a dangerous business, Frodo, going out your door. You step onto the road, and if you do not keep your feet, there's no knowing where you might be swept off to." Young military officers are encouraged to take bold, decisive action, and the same is true in a business context. When you do not constantly move toward your vision, you let others shape your destiny. Even if you fail, it is better to move forward, assess what went wrong, and implement what you learned. If you do this, the recognition and promotions will come to you *and* your people. This is a recipe for continued success as long as you realize that it was the teamwork you established that got you there.

I believe a mistake that many leaders in organizations, companies, government, and even the military forget at times is that they are dealing with people. We have so many metrics and numbers involved in determining our success that it becomes a full-time job just to chart and graph how those numbers reflect our success. It becomes too easy to forget that it is people that ultimately bring about success or failure. Including humility in your personal leadership style mandates that you constantly strive for a good working relationship with your staff, and that you will do your best to look to their needs.

I hope that you see by now that the central themes we have explored in regard to leadership constantly integrate with each other. Putting your people first, communicating clearly, promoting teamwork, balancing out humility and confidence, etc. All these are necessary and feed into one another. A good leader tries to keep in mind all these elements in building his team and working toward goals. That is a successful formula to follow no matter what your leadership role may be.

The next two chapters are not going to deal with specific leadership skills. Rather, these chapters will explore important components of being a well-rounded leader. Again, it all comes down to people. You are a person. As a person, there are things you can do with your life that will make you a more effective and successful leader. We explore some of those now.

KEY TAKEAWAYS

1. Many people who claim to be self-made success stories actually benefited from others in many different ways.

2. Sometimes you may never know about the positive effects of your actions on others around you, but this should not deter you from always trying to help them.

3. Never miss an opportunity to pay somebody a compliment or tell her that you appreciate something about her.

In this chapter, Corporal Adam Hart described an incident at the 611 Bridge. I was always nervous when we went there because the site was not very well protected, as you can see in this picture.

I am truly lucky to be married to Dahlia, my best friend and closest confidant. Our wedding was the happiest day of my life.

CHAPTER 13

ENJOY YOUR FRIENDS AND FAMILY

OUR WORK IS IMPORTANT. It allows us to pay bills and support our families and ourselves. Ideally, you have a job that you truly enjoy. Ideally, you strive to do your best in that job every day. If you own your business, you have a deeply vested interest in making your company a success. The American work ethic is to work hard, and most people, especially those in any leadership position, do exactly that.

However, to do better at your job and to be truly successful in life, you have to understand that your job is only one component of your being. As some of you have probably already realized, it would be easy for a business owner or manager to get so wrapped up at work that they forget their life is made up of people *outside* of the work-place. Work becomes so important and all-consuming that they may overlook their spouses, significant others, children, family, and friends.

I can definitively say that I would not be where I am now, after my injury, if it were not for my wife, Dahlia. Hundreds of people worked on me and helped me to recover, but she has been my anchor. She has kept everything together for me. You can have all of the leadership skills in the world, but you need love and support from someone outside of the workplace to help keep everything in perspective.

It is specifically because of the injury that caused my physical, mental, and emotional issues that I am far closer to Dahlia than I would have thought possible. I know that I am far stronger than I ever would have been alone. I can now put everyday obstacles into their proper perspective and focus on what is truly important to Dahlia and me. Just as you want to promote the concept of "we" and not "I" within your employee team, you want to use that same philosophy when you are close to someone. Having her in my life has shaped the decisions I have made since being shot—always for the better.

Dahlia and I met in 2006 at a Spanish immersion course in Buenos Aires, Argentina. Dahlia was there from California, and I came from Virginia. We were in the same small class, and although I was only there for three weeks, we really hit it off during that short time. One afternoon while in Argentina, I took Dahlia to a restaurant that was famous for its grilled meat. She ordered seafood, but I ordered a meal typically designed for two people that consisted of all sorts of barbequed meat. As a Marine captain, I figured what better way to impress this young woman than to show her how much red meat I could eat!

I did not realize, then, that Dahlia is a vegetarian. Needless to say, she was not too impressed with my eating prowess, especially when I fell into a food coma about an hour later. For some reason, though, she gave me a second chance.

We dated that summer back in the States, and when I deployed to Iraq, Dahlia left to pursue her PhD at Cambridge University in England. Unlike earlier wars, it is much easier to stay in touch when one person is in a war zone. We were able to communicate practically every day through email, letters and packages, and the occasional satellite phone call.

After my 70 mph drive down IED-infested streets, and my helo ride to Balad while "packaged" in a body bag, packed with gauze and wrapped naked, but tightly so no part of me fell out of place (one of my doctors told me I was "butt naked, but toasty warm"), the military airlifted me out of Iraq. They took me to the military hospital in Landstuhl, Germany. Because of the distance from the US, it was unusual for injured service members to receive personal visits there. However, it was fairly easy for Dahlia to get to me from England. I was there for four days, and when they sent me on to the naval hospital in Bethesda, Maryland, Dahlia decided to leave her doctoral program to be with me in the hospital. Because of the distance from the US, it was unusual for injured service members to receive personal visits there. However, it was fairly easy for Dahlia to get to me from England. I was there for four days, and when they sent me on to the Naval hospital in Bethesda, Maryland, Dahlia decided to leave her doctoral program to be with me in the hospital.

Never mind that studying at Cambridge had been a lifelong dream of hers. And never mind that she did not know anyone near the hospital. Or that, at that point, the doctors did not even know if I would survive. It is very rare for someone to live after that kind of gunshot wound. When I awoke from my coma, however, Dahlia was there. Together, we have incorporated every aspect of teamwork into our relationship. My recovery would not have been so successful if it were not for the two of us working together.

To give you a small idea of how we worked together, one of my milestones was when I bit into a tiny hamburger slider that Dahlia made for me. This was after I received my upper dentures. For the first time in six years, I was able to bite into food. Up until that point, I had to cut food up very small and shove it into the back of my mouth where I still had a couple of molars to chew. My vegetarian wife prepared me the hamburger so I could actually take a bite out of something. It had to be something small because the scar tissue in my mouth does not allow me to open up very widely. Can you imagine going six years without biting into an apple, a slice of pizza, a hamburger, or a thousand other things?

I can. So Dahlia's hamburger is something I will never forget—a milestone in my recovery, but so much more than that because of her.

Eating is not always the enjoyable experience it once was, especially with my diminished sense of taste and smell. I wear a bib with every meal so I do not make a complete mess of my clothes. Despite my best efforts, it is still practically impossible for me to eat without spilling food and drink all over myself. I know it probably looks pretty goofy, especially at work events. However, meals are now a special occasion for Dahlia and me because I know she tries so hard to cook me food that is both flavorful enough for me to enjoy and soft enough that it does not hurt the inside of my very sensitive, rebuilt mouth.

Dahlia and I were married in 2008, and I cannot imagine life without her. We fully support each other professionally and personally, and I know I can always count on her. Although I tell Dahlia before any of my surgeries now that she does not need to be there, that all the tough ones are behind me, she still comes to each one. She will not hear any of that and insists on being there with me. The truth is that I actually do feel so much calmer and relaxed with her beside me, and I love having her be the last person I see before I am wheeled into the operating room. And now that I have written this, she knows that and will feel obligated to come to each. (Sorry, Dahlia, but I like having you there!)

I am also incredibly proud of Dahlia. She has achieved wild success as a third-grade teacher. Not only was she selected as the Teacher of the Year at her elementary school, but for all of Arlington County in Northern Virginia, as well. Although Dahlia always wanted to get back to Cambridge University, we are now heading to Columbia University in New York City so she can pursue her PhD there, which is very exciting. She inspires me with her commitment to her students, to social justice, and to the underprivileged in society who often do not have a voice of their own. I will always treasure Dahlia's critical support of my recovery, but our relationship is now so much deeper than that.

Still today, when I am experiencing moments of PTS and cannot get certain images out of my mind, she is there for me. In fact, when Dahlia and I identified that I had PTS, we tackled it together. She is a big reason that I did not retreat into myself when dealing with it, and she encouraged me to seek out the help I needed.

Not everyone is going to have this type of relationship in his life—I know that. I'm not saying, "Go find your Dahlia." Though you should certainly hold on if you do. What I am saying is that almost everyone has one or two people they are close with, whether they be family or friends. These are the connections to keep you grounded to the world outside of work. We all need someone to laugh with and talk to outside of the workplace. If you do not, you have a very unhealthy balance in your life. You know the saying that "All work and no play makes Jack a dull boy?" Well, not only does it make Jack dull, but it also gives him stress, anxiety, meager social skills, and the makings of a poor leader.

I had an epiphany while on vacation with Dahlia, recently. We were on the West Coast. (Of course, it was not a complete vacation because I was doing some work while I was out there. Unfortunately, that is the reality for a lot of us. The upside is that it has forced me to think a lot about incorporating a better work-life balance into my schedule—something I encourage very much and have not mastered in the slightest, though I have a plan, which you will see below.) We went to a place that I can best describe as an outdoor spa. On our way out there, I talked with Dahlia about trying to do some yoga in the mornings. I had read a number of articles about the benefits of yoga for men and for wounded warriors, but I had not attempted it yet. After our visit there, however, I was a convert. I was firmly committed to establishing a healthy and holistic work-life balance. Just as leadership is important in business, I recognized that it would take personal leadership to bring about a successful balance.

Our afternoon there was such a refreshing experience. First off, the spa included a steam room, a sauna, various sunny sitting areas, and a number of pools ranging from frigid cold to very hot. The spa does not allow talking there, so it is completely silent. Whether you want to or not, you will quietly contemplate what is going on in your life, address your challenges, analyze your successes, and think about your priorities. Hopefully, you will also relax and think about nothing at all, at times.

Moving from the steam room to the sauna to the cold pool to the 104-degree hot tub not only left me feeling clean, relaxed, and with a renewed sense of energy, but it also left me wondering how I could incorporate something like this into my daily life. Like with anything else in life and business, I have to take charge of this plan or it will never happen. Here are some of my ideas:

1. I already exercise regularly, but I will also include various classes, such as spinning and abs, in my regimen because I work out harder in a group environment.

2. Before I start work in the morning, I will spend time in quiet solitude. If nice weather permits, this will be in my backyard or on my patio. This will be a short period of reflection and contemplation, where I will think about what I want to accomplish that day and what my immediate and long-term goals are. Once I start working, I simply will not have an opportunity for that meditation.

3. I will start taking some yoga classes. Not only will the physical health aspects of yoga be good for me, especially since I am not very limber, but the mental aspect will help too. One thing I learned during my recovery is that our mental outlook is so important to our successes (as well as our downfalls), and yoga certainly helps with that.

4. I will pick a time to stop working. I run my own business and work from home, so I do not have a "typical" work schedule. It is not unusual for me to send emails late into the evening, but I do not know how helpful that really is to me or to those to whom I am sending the emails. My goal will be to stop working at 7:00 p.m., and to make a list of everything I want to accomplish the next day. That way, my brain will think about those things while I sleep.

5. I will ensure that the way I spend my time matches up with my priorities. For example, if I determine that my top three priorities are my family, my business, and my continued recovery from my injury, but I spend half of my day responding to incoming emails, I will never make any progress toward achieving the right balance, with family first. Therefore, I will take the time to list out my top three to five priorities. I will include my short and long-term goals. I will then write out how I can best focus on those priorities and achieve my goals, and structure my schedule accordingly.

I realized from my brief vacation that I needed to plan more "me" time in my schedule as well as "us" time for Dahlia and me. I found the quiet solitude very peaceful—just me and my thoughts. This is what it has come down to for many of us. If we do not make ourselves, our family, friends, and outside interests a priority, they will slowly get pushed aside by the demands of work.

A very successful executive I know plans his calendar for the year every August. He uses that time of the year because he has a bunch of kids and that is when he usually receives the school schedules. The first thing he puts on the calendar is his wife's birthday and their anniversary (very smart man!). He then adds the kids' birthdays and those school events he wants to be part of: parent-teacher conferences, graduations, etc. He sprinkles in other family items like vacations and holidays. Then, he starts to put in the important dates for work. As he told me:

> *"Certain family events are such a high priority that work has to fit around them. When I have to set up meetings with business-related people, I do not sacrifice the important dates. If I can't make a meeting because it conflicts with one of those dates, I just say I have something important that I cannot reschedule. The other person does not have to know what it is. It prevents adding any extra stress or anxiety at home. After all, when you have days like that at work, you do get to leave at the end of the day. You do not generally have that option at home!"*

He is right. You want your time outside of work to be pleasant, even fun. It is so much easier to tackle a new day in the workplace when you go in feeling relaxed and happy. If you allow work to screw up your outside relationships, then you are setting out on a never-ending merry-go-round of grief. Work will became an unceasing grind, and you will have no outlets in which to relax and to help keep life in perspective.

You can see this manifest itself when you encounter a proud workaholic. They wear it as a badge of honor that they come in before anyone and stay the latest. They figure that must make them better than anyone else in the company and they adopt that attitude (a particular brand of the arrogance discussed earlier). Furthermore, they believe that anyone who works for them should take on these same workaholic tendencies.

The problem with this entire premise is that most workaholics fall into a pattern of diminishing returns. It is a proven fact that a person becomes less productive the longer that she works. It actually gets to the point that a person can become counterproductive and do more harm than good when working too long.

There are going to be projects and days where you need to put in long hours. That is always going to happen. What I am talking about, here, is when someone habitually puts in very long hours on the job. When that occurs, everything is going to suffer. It hurts the company, the workaholic's health, and the people who work for him and her—in short, it hurts the whole team.

As a leader in your company, you need to know the difference between work and activity. An example of this is when the owner of a company would brag about how he was on his computer at 6:00 a.m. to 9:00 p.m. every day. He looked at this as working hard for the company he was trying to get off the ground. The problem was that he spent a lot of time reading emails, surfing the Internet, and working on easy projects that were way down on the priority scale. If he had spent half that time devoted to the matters that needed his attention, his business may have gotten off the ground instead of crashing and burning.

Do you realize that, as a leader of others, you owe it to your company and to your people to keep a good balance between work and the rest of your life? A leader who does maintain that balance is much more effective. They come to work energized and ready to put all of the leadership skills we have talked about into practice. People who put an effort into having a good life outside of work tend to be physically, emotionally, and spiritually healthier than someone who lives their work 24/7.

A leader who maintains a good work-life balance is much better at making sure her staff does the same thing, too. She understands the importance of such a balance. She will notice if a worker is spending too much time at the office and needs to take a break. This type of leader encourages her people to take their vacation time and does not make someone feel guilty for taking the time they earned. (Yes, sadly this does happen!) A great leader knows that the staff has to be healthy and happy to be productive. I am sure you have noticed by now how often this concept of communication and knowing your staff comes into play for a successful leader. If you only remember one thing, remember the importance of knowing and communicating with those around you.

Tough times at work are inevitable no matter how much you love your job. Things often happen beyond your control. I enjoyed being an officer in the Marines, but something totally out of my control changed my situation. Likewise, you could get a new boss at work who decides he wants to bring in his own people. Suddenly, you find yourself demoted or out the door. You may have been a great manager, but circumstances brought about an unwelcome change. The people who cannot handle these down-turns tend to be the ones who have no balance to their work. They have no close relationships outside of the office. They may not pursue any interests or hobbies. Work becomes their life. When things are that out of whack, the ability to handle any huge workplace disasters is extremely limited.

I am so grateful to have Dahlia in my life. She has made everything I have achieved possible since life turned upside down on me in Iraq. If there is not a family member or friend that you are close to, maybe it is time to make that one of your priorities. If you have no passions or interests outside of work, perhaps you should take some of your accumulated vacation time and see what gets your motor going. For my part, that Spanish immersion course in Buenos Aires changed my life for the better. It may seem sacrilegious to your way of thinking that something can be more important than work. However, you will find that you will become a better leader and a better, happier person if you lead a balanced life.

KEY TAKEAWAYS

1. Take the time to list out your priorities in life—include topics outside of work!

2. Relationships are critical to our well-being—make the time to invest in them.

3. Strong leaders understand the need for time off, for themselves and their employees.

For us, part of our work-life balance is saving time for great vacations. Several years ago we visited Ireland and took this picture together at the Cliffs of Moher.

I have been fortunate enough to lead a team at the US Chamber of Commerce Foundation's Hiring Our Heroes campaign. My team focuses on employment opportunities for wounded veterans and caregivers.

CHAPTER 14

BE A GREAT CITIZEN

AS WE EXPLORED IN the last chapter, maintaining a healthy work-life balance is an important part of being an effective leader. You need more than just work in your life to be happy and productive. When you are taking care of yourself so that you can approach your job in the healthiest way possible, you are going to do so much better in any role, especially a leadership role where your example matters so much.

There is one more aspect of being a business leader that you should consider. If you have reached such a position, it means that you have many good qualities and traits that another organization can use. You should not be afraid to get out and use your talents to help a cause or group that you believe in. This could manifest in many ways, from being a coach for a Little League team to volunteering at your church to running for the town council.

America is full of opportunities for you to be of help to others. There is so much good that we would be missing if it were not for the millions of volunteers who participate in the organizations that they support. All you have to do is look around your community, and you will find many places that are begging for someone with leadership talents to help them along.

I have found that a good part of my life has been devoted to organizations I can identify with. I have been and continue to be more than happy to lend a hand to them whenever I can. I want to share some of the causes for which I am very passionate. I want to do this to get you thinking about what makes you feel the same way. I hope my enthusiasm is contagious. I also want to educate you a little on a few of my heartfelt projects.

I am sure that it is no surprise to the reader that I am a big supporter of veterans. In my role talking to corporate leadership, I continually promote the hiring of veterans. You see, when we talk about one of today's veterans, especially one who signed up after 9/11, we are talking about someone who signed a blank check to our country. That check says that she was prepared to pay whatever price necessary to ensure our way of life here at home. You could have a veteran who might never have deployed, or one who deployed eight times. In a veteran, you have someone trained in the toughest possible environments, but who might not be able to find a career that takes advantage of her particular talents when they leave the military.

We all know that today's veterans are coming out of the military with an incredible array of skills and abilities. Many of them worked in tech-related fields, and just about everybody has served in some sort of leadership capacity. They know the value of teamwork, yet they are used to taking the initiative when appropriate. They also have experience making important decisions in the blink of an eye. Each has been an important part of teams that had to work long hours to accomplish a mission and meet hard deadlines.

These veterans will show up for work on time. They will do what you tell them. They will take the initiative when appropriate. And they will not quit until they finish the job. This is the message I try to get across to the companies and business people I meet. I do not think it is right that veterans have a higher unemployment rate than their civilian counterparts. At the same time, I think that having a fulfilling career is one of the most therapeutic parts of a successful transition out of the military, and in my case, adaption to a "new normal."

As you have seen by now, getting shot in the head left me with many physical issues. I always respected people who had to use handicapped parking, but it is a lot different when I am the one pulling into the blue space. I never thought much about people with disabilities before I was one of them. When I was stationed in Japan, I never saw a disabled person. But it was not that there were not any. It was because the government often kept them hidden from the public. As a little kid, I lived in Vienna, Austria, for a time. There was a special school near our house for all the kids with disabilities. There was no integration at all. After my experience, it became a natural concern for me to take an interest in people dealing with disabilities, generally, and wounded veterans in particular.

I do think that our local and strong national programs for people with disabilities need to work more with our wounded warrior groups to integrate the two. This could be happening already, but the fact that I have not really heard about it probably says a lot. Sometimes, I think about the amputees from the wars in Iraq and Afghanistan who went to the hospitals in Boston to visit and motivate the injured patients there after the bombing at the 2013 Boston Marathon. After tragedy, when those victims were facing some of the hard questions I had to ask, too, I know it was comforting and motivating to see those wounded warriors come through with success stories. It is in times like that when I see so many opportunities for the wounded warrior and the civilian disabled population to work together.

For me, one big issue has been dealing with change. For those who enjoy the status quo, change is scary. As we talked about earlier in the book, I have learned that change is good. In my case, I have become a much more compassionate person than I was before. During my recovery, I have had to fill out hundreds of medical and insurance forms, and that is always frustrating. One day, though, I thought about how miserable it must be if you were not very good at reading and writing. Because of that simple passing thought, I started to volunteer in Washington DC at the Literacy Center to help adults learn how to read and write better.

Frankly, I do not know if I would have been involved with this effort if it were not for my injury. I recently completed an advanced law degree at Georgetown University, and I would drive by a homeless shelter on my way home. I always saw many men and women just kind of hanging out there, all quietly suffering in their own worlds. Perhaps before my injury, I may have wondered why they just did not go get a job, any job, and move on with their lives. I was wrong. Now I understand that the majority of them are probably struggling with some sort of mental illness. And as someone with PTS, I instead wonder if they are getting the care that they need and deserve.

Because of what I went through, I am also a part of a number of different wounded warrior organizations committed to helping so many of our returning heroes and their spouses. I derive a lot of satisfaction from that, and I know that I would not be doing this kind of advocacy if it were not for my injury. It sounds crazy, but this change—so violently thrust upon me—and all that comes with it have actually been very beneficial to me in the long run. My life is far richer now than before I deployed to Iraq.

Sometimes we think we are too busy to spend more time helping an organization we say we care about. I suggest keeping your eyes and ears open. Something may touch you in a way that you never thought it could. Very often, it does not take much to really make a difference. There may be one night or one event for an organization where you can devote some time. That may be enough to make it a success. All you have to do is to be aware of what is happening out there in the world and your community.

For example, I love my job giving inspirational speeches. I am fortunate enough to travel around the country and speak with a wide variety of corporations about leadership, overcoming adversity, the upside of change, and the lessons I learned during the recovery process after my injury in Iraq. As a byproduct of talking with many individuals after those presentations, I often hear about significant difficulties they are struggling with in their own lives.

I spoke recently at a charity golf tournament that was raising money to support a number of nonprofit organizations dedicated to helping wounded warriors and their families. While there, I heard one particularly sad story that has stayed with me. In fact, it was far more than sad: It was heavy, woeful, and tear-jerking. I will repeat it here, but am sure I cannot do justice to the story I heard.

A woman was talking about veteran suicide. Many have heard that 22 veterans commit suicide every day, and while that number may actually be somewhat consistent with the rest of American society, something about it jumps off the page. Maybe we think our veterans simply do not fall into that category of "suicidal people." We believe that our veterans are strong and resilient due to their service (although that same service exposes them to such challenging conditions) or that a wide variety of resources exist for our nation's veterans who do face suicidal thoughts. The truth is that many veterans actually do not know about the resources that exist. Others may have had a bad experience with one and have given up.

This woman told us that she spoke at a premier university about her service dog initiative. At the end of her presentation, an audience member stood and related his story. He was the proud father of a young service member who had deployed to Iraq. He noticed that when his son came back, he was different from the young man who had left. The soldier would not talk with his family about what he had seen and experienced overseas, although they could tell that it weighed heavily on him. They encouraged him to talk with them, but he always refused, staying silent. Over time, the situation deteriorated to the point where the father called the suicide crisis hotline and, in his words, "an angel was on the other end of the phone line." The counselor spoke with him and his son and it seemed like things were going to be okay.

The father was later sitting on the couch, reflecting on the phone conversation. He looked up and noticed that his son was watching him from the doorway. Suddenly his son started crying. The son asked his father to hold him the way he used to. The father explained to the audience that he did exactly that. He held his son for 43 minutes.

Then he held him again the next day when he cut him down from the ceiling rafter in his son's room.

The father had no idea that evening was the last time he would hold his son. He had no idea that would be their last conversation. He thought they had made real progress with the phone call and that his son was on the path to recovery. I cried in front of 200 people listening to that story. It was devastating to hear about this young veteran, physically returned from overseas, who felt that taking his own life was his best option.

You hear stories like this and you feel prompted to act. I believe Americans feel that they can make a difference. It does not have to be tragedy like this that motivates you. You may see an organization that works hard at making life better for children or senior citizens, and you may want to help. You can help with your time, your money, the resources of your company, or a combination of all three. The important thing is that if you hear about something that speaks to you, then **get involved** with it!

After hearing that story about the young veteran's suicide, I try to do what I can to promote awareness of the situation and the available services to combat it. There are many programs designed to defeat the staggering number of veteran suicides. Many of these programs are saving our service members, one person at a time. They focus on outdoor recreation, individual counseling, peer mentoring, equine therapy, service dogs, and any number of other methods. I simply ask that you support the groups in your local communities pushing forward on these programs or initiatives. It can be as easy as playing in a charity golf tournament or making a monthly commitment.

No question about it, though, it is a matter of life or death.

Another connected cause I give time to is for those caregivers of wounded veterans. Although I am a wounded warrior and my wife served as my caregiver during the first several years of my recovery, I certainly did not appreciate the full scope of the problems these caregivers face. If I did not recognize this as a major problem in our society—as a wounded warrior married to a devoted caregiver—how could the rest of America?

I recently had the honor of serving as the master of ceremonies for a caregiver networking reception held at the U.S. Chamber of Commerce in conjunction with the Elizabeth Dole Foundation. The event was certainly a success: Over 30 military caregivers had the opportunity to talk directly with employers from national corporations who want to hire caregivers at locations around the country.

The attendees listened to a panel discussion focused on best practices for corporations supporting the specific needs of many of our caregivers, including flexible work schedules and work-from-home opportunities. Additionally, they listened to how caregivers can incorporate into their resumes the skills that they have developed while caring for their wounded warriors. Perhaps most illuminating, however, was some of the information that Senator Elizabeth Dole and the U.S. Chamber of Commerce President and CEO Tom Donahue stressed, which is the incredible and unique challenges faced by this generation of military caregivers.

We learned that a whopping 1.1 million caregivers are caring for post-9/11 veterans. These veterans tend to be younger and are not part of a support network. We also learned that military caregivers as a whole consistently experience worse health issues, greater strains in family relationships, and more workplace issues than non-caregivers. However, the post-9/11 military caregivers fare the worst in these areas.

Again, this would not have been an issue with me if it did not relate to something I experienced. Our communities are filled with good people who can donate some of their talents. The United States has not been around all these years just because of the efforts of government and business. Many of our values and strengths took center stage because Americans wanted to be good citizens and do what they could for the common good.

I feel like I have been given a gift, still being alive, and that I have a second lease on life. My experiences since that day being struck down in Iraq have ignited my passion to help where I can. I believe we should all feel that way. If you are ever in a position to help another person or organization or your community, do it. Our towns and cities are full of people who need help. Poverty, sickness, and ignorance unleash a toll on people. It is up to those who can help, to help. After all, if those who can lend a hand do not, what will happen to the America we know? Needless to say, I have been the lucky recipient of many small acts of kindness.

Right after I arrived in the hospital, one of my best friends, Jay Town, came up from Alabama to visit me. Jay knew that Dahlia had been spending 18-hour days at the hospital and needed a break. Jay and I had been very close in the Marine Corps, and because he had not deployed to Iraq, I think he felt particularly anguished about what had happened to me. And that was not easy duty for Jay in the hospital. My face at that time almost looked inhuman because of how swollen it was. But Jay took over right where Dahlia had left off: Every 15 minutes or so he used the suction machine to clean my mouth, wiped away the blood that kept leaking out of me, and made sure I was as comfortable as possible. He even spent a couple of nights sleeping in the armchair in my room just so I would not be alone.

Also, another good friend of mine, Mike Murphy, whom I had known since our freshman year of college almost 20 years earlier, came by to visit Dahlia and me on a regular basis, even though he lived 50 miles away and had to drive through a lot of traffic to get to me. At the time, Mike, who was married with three children, was also juggling work, coaching a high school rugby team and many other activities. And the timing of one of his visits could not have been more fortuitous. I was in the middle of one of my hallucinations and explaining to Dahlia that the picture of flowers on the wall was really a picture from a rugby game and that the players were talking to me. Mike and I had actually played together in the college rugby game I was referencing, and although Dahlia had no idea what I was talking about, Mike was able to have a long conversation with me about each of the players and what they were currently doing in life. And Mike also made a huge impression on the staff there. On one of his visits, he brought a huge box of bagels for the nurses and support staff, and they really appreciated that.

And I will never forget the tender care and support provided by Mr. and Mrs. Zachariasiewicz. I had graduated from law school with their son (Zach), and he and I were very close. I had always enjoyed spending time with Mr. and Mrs. Z, but of course never had any idea how important they would be to Dahlia and me after I was shot. By amazing coincidence, Mr. and Mrs. Z lived just a couple of miles away from the hospital, so they invited Dahlia to stay with them while I was in Bethesda. Not only was this incredibly generous of them, but absolutely critical to Dahlia's health. If she had not had such a motherly woman looking after her and ensuring that she was sleeping enough and eating the right food, Dahlia very easily could have spent every moment in the hospital, losing sight of the fact that her own health was just as important as mine. In fact, when I was having a particularly horrifying hallucination, Mr. Z sat through it with me for several hours late into the night just to let me know that he was there and everything was going to be all right.

If the situation presents itself, take advantage of the opportunity to act like Jay, Mike, and Mr. and Mrs. Zachariasiewicz (and many others). The funny thing is that when you talk to most people who give their time to a cause or organization, they feel like they received more out of helping than what they gave. That is okay. It is no sin to feel good about doing the right thing.

KEY TAKEAWAYS

1. Even in America, so many people need help with regard to the most basic aspects of life. Volunteering is a great way to help others who are not as fortunate as you.

2. Before you volunteer, take the time to identify groups or causes that really speak to you—this will help ensure a much better experience for you and those you help.

3. When I needed it the most, so many people offered to help, and some of them were absolutely critical to my recovery. Never miss an opportunity to fill that role.

Volunteer opportunities abound across our country. I really enjoyed this opportunity in New York City to work with other volunteers from Give An Hour to build a community garden.

CHAPTER 15

GO FOR IT

IN THE MARINE CORPS, we each receive incredibly detailed directives on how to use our rifles. Instructors drill into you how to break them down, the proper way to clean them, what ammunition to use, how to care for them in the field, etc. You get to the point where you can take that rifle apart and put it back together blindfolded. All of this training is great, but it does not really come together until you are at the firing range and shooting at targets to see if you can actually hit anything. And then, of course, you have the real thing.

This book is a lot like that process. We went over many different pieces of what it means to be a leader and the proper way to conduct yourself in that role. I caution you not to look at all of the various concepts we have discussed as independent from one another. You do not have to juggle all of the parts of being a leader with the idea that you pluck one out of the air when you need it. Instead, you have to assemble all of the separate components in order to become a successful leader. Then you need to actually get out there, use this model, and lead!

As I bring this book to a close, I want to review with you 10 notable quotes on leadership. They are a good way to illustrate the practical applications of all that you have read. My desire is that the lessons I talk about in this book give you the confidence to go out into your company and put them into practice.

No man will make a great leader who wants to do it all himself, or to get all the credit for doing it.

— Andrew Carnegie

The essence of leadership is not the title or the trappings that may come with the position. It is the ability to successfully lead others to meet the desired goals and objectives. Once you get a promotion that puts you into a new leadership role, enjoy that moment. Then put your ego aside, roll up your sleeves, and get to work. You need to get your people functioning as a unit and moving forward together. Once you have done your part, getting them to work as a well-oiled machine, the sky is the limit as to what the team can accomplish. If you train your people well, then they will never look at you as a micro-manager. You must train them and then trust them to do their jobs. You do not have to be looking over everyone's shoulder on a day-to-day basis.

You manage things; you lead people.

— Rear Admiral Grace Murray Hopper

You never hear someone say about George Washington, "He was a good manager," or about a star quarterback as "a great field supervisor." No, the word "leader" is always used. No matter if you are the CEO or manager or any other particular title, you have to think of yourself as a leader. The people who report to you come to you for your leadership. They are looking to you for guidance, direction, and decision-making. Nothing is as demoralizing to an employee as when they go to their supervisor with a question and do not get an answer. Even, "I don't know, but I will find out" is a perfectly acceptable answer—especially as opposed to no answer, or worse, a fabricated response. You have a responsibility to your superiors and the people who report to you to lead.

As we look ahead into the next century, leaders will be those who empower others.

— Bill Gates

Remember that one of your duties as a supervisor is to train your people to become leaders in their own right. You are only going to hurt yourself if you do not allow those under you the opportunity to grow and progress in their jobs. They are not in competition with you. If you have that insecurity, you need either to get over it or find a new line of work. You have to remember that if you are doing the right things and your people are getting their own promotions as your group is exceeding all of its goals, then your bosses are going to notice your work, too. That is only going to open up more doors for you to move up the corporate ladder.

Not the cry, but the flight of a wild duck, leads the flock to fly and follow.

— Chinese Proverb

You always have to set the example. How you conduct yourself in your position is going to have a bearing on how your people respond to you. You have to be very careful to make sure your actions back up everything you say to your staff. Not too many things can erode respect for a leader more than if her people detect hypocrisy in the leader's action. It can be as simple as telling your staff to be on time and you, yourself, always being 15 minutes late. It is painful to watch when you can see someone's leadership base begin to erode. While a true leader can turn such a problem around by making a concerted effort to change, it is so much easier never to drift into that difficulty. Let your people always see that you mean what you say and that you are consistent in your actions. Remember, you only get one chance to make a first impression.

The growth and development of people is the highest calling of leadership.

— Harvey Firestone

Do you notice how we continually come around to a leader's ability to help her people get better at their own jobs? In the Marines, everything we did was to encourage men and women to become better

Marines, in general, as well as to master their particular assignments. That should be your mission at work. You want your people to become even more valued employees to the company by knowing and being the best at their jobs. If you make this your focus, you will discover that all of your goals and success seem to follow naturally. That is because you are focusing on your people. When you do that, everything else falls into place.

> *My own definition of leadership is this: The capacity and the will to rally men and women to a common purpose and the character which inspires confidence.*
>
> — General Montgomery

This is a good example of how you have to look at the qualities of leadership as a whole, instead of leadership's component parts. While you are working on getting your people to be the best they can be, you are also doing this in the context of getting them to buy into the idea that everyone is working toward the same objectives. I see football as a wonderful illustration of this. You have 11 players with specific responsibilities. Each player has a high degree of difficulty in terms of their particular position and the athleticism that is called for. For the play to go well, though, all 11 players need to perform almost perfectly and synchronously for the team to move forward. In the Marines, a battlefield situation comes together in the same manner. Many Marines have to do their own jobs well in order to achieve the battlefield objective. Your job as a business leader is to improve everyone's individual performance and to make certain that each of the individuals understand that they are also working jointly toward a common goal. You are the glue that will hold all of this together as they look up to you.

> *If your actions inspire others to dream more, learn more, do more and become more, you are a leader.*
>
> — John Quincy Adams

Once again, we are reminded that a good leader concentrates on what he does with his people. It is actually hard to find any quotes on leadership that pat the leader on the back without taking into account the leader's followers. Your people are the priority. They eat first. And you work with them to help them become top-notch in their jobs. If you look at ineffective leaders in the workplace, this is where they usually fail. They were more concerned with how they would look to their bosses, rather than worrying about the people who report to them. They did not understand that their bosses would think better of them if they exercised great leadership for their people and motivated the team forward.

> *The best executive is the one who has sense enough*
> *to pick good men to do what he wants done, and self-*
> *restraint enough to keep from meddling with them while*
> *they do it.*
>
> — Theodore Roosevelt

There is a saying among jockeys that if you have a great racehorse, just let him run. You do some training with the horse and guide him through the pack out of the gate, but when you have an open lane in front, let that horse do what he does best. A good leader does the same thing with his people. Your goal as a leader is to get your people to know their job well so that you and the rest of the team can trust them to do it. The flip side of this is that your people know they have your trust, which builds up their own confidence in performing their job well. When you get your team to this point, a leader needs to avoid the insecurity of constantly checking on her team. As a leader, you need to keep apprised on how everyone is doing, but if you are constantly micromanaging them, your people are going to think you doubt their abilities. They, in turn, may start doubting themselves. Before you know it, you are back at square one and have to work harder to get everyone believing in themselves again.

Leaders aren't born, they are made. And they are made just like anything else, through hard work. And that's the price we'll have to pay to achieve that goal, or any goal.

— Vince Lombardi

The Marines do not bring young men and women into the Corps with the expectation that they stay privates for their entire careers. It would be kind of tough going into battle without any leaders. Therefore, the Marines have a deliberate methodology for developing our leaders of the future. A good business, no matter its size, needs to do the same thing. Just as most leaders do not spring out of nothingness, a business is not going to develop leaders if it does not make it a priority. You may be surprised at how many companies have to look to the outside to replace existing leadership. Usually, sadly, the simple explanation for that is because they never concentrated on training their existing people to be leaders. You need to recognize this where you work and take appropriate steps to change the culture, even if it is only within your own sphere of responsibilities. When you are helping your people to become leaders, you are moving the company forward.

Never doubt that a small group of thoughtful, concerned citizens can change the world. Indeed, it is the only thing that ever has.

— Margaret Mead

To me, this quote illustrates a couple of important points. One, a leader can come from any background if she has the desire to make a difference. If you have the desire, then you can learn the right techniques and apply them. The second point backs up what I said in chapter 14 about being a good citizen. Many good things in America have come from the "concerned citizens" that Ms. Mead talks about. If your talents have propelled you to a successful point of leadership in business, then please use those same gifts to help your community and your country. That is how America became the great country she is today. It is going to take the continued efforts of people with concern, vision, and leadership to help our towns, states, and country continue to grow and be the land of opportunity we still believe the United States to be.

I want to thank you so much for reading this book. Hopefully, it gave you a new perspective on leadership that you can use. No matter what is going on around you, do not stop asking for help, do not stop helping others, and keep striving to make a difference at work and in your communities. I know that your jobs can be stressful—it seems like everyone works in a highly competitive field these days. But I want to impress on you how important it is to maintain a good sense of humor. If you keep your sense of humor and apply these lessons of leadership, you will go far. Semper Fi!

30590226R00102

Made in the USA
San Bernardino, CA
17 February 2016